Walk the Walk

The Second Coming of Steve Jobs

A Tale of Two Valleys

Change or Die

Walk the Walk

The #1 Rule for Real Leaders

ALAN DEUTSCHMAN

Portfolio

PORTFOLIO

Published by the Penguin Group

Penguin Group (USA) Inc., 375 Hudson Street, New York, New York 10014, U.S.A. · Penguin Group (Canada), 90 Eglinton Avenue East, Suite 700, Toronto, Ontario, Canada M4P 2Y3 (a division of Pearson Penguin Canada Inc.) · Penguin Books Ltd., 80 Strand, London WC2R 0RL, England · Penguin Ireland, 25 St. Stephen's Green, Dublin 2, Ireland (a division of Penguin Books Ltd.) · Penguin Books Australia Ltd, 250 Camberwell Road, Camberwell, Victoria 3124, Australia (a division of Pearson Australia Group Pty. Ltd.) · Penguin Books India Pvt Ltd, 11 Community Centre, Panchsheel Park, New Delhi - 110 017, India · Penguin Group (NZ), 67 Apollo Drive, Rosedale, North Shore 0632, New Zealand (a division of Pearson New Zealand Ltd) · Penguin Books (South Africa) (Pty) Ltd, 24 Sturdee Avenue, Rosebank, Johannesburg 2196, South Africa

Penguin Books Ltd, Registered Offices: 80 Strand, London WC2R 0RL, England

First published in 2009 by Portfolio, a member of Penguin Group (USA) Inc.
First Printing, September 2009

10 9 8 7 6 5 4 3 2 1

LIBRARY OF CONGRESS CATALOGING IN PUBLICATION DATA
Deutschman, Alan, date.
   Walk the walk: the #1 rule for real leaders/Alan Deutschman.
      p.   cm.
   Includes bibliographical references and index.
   ISBN 978-1-59184-278-1
   1. Leadership.   1.   Title.
   HD57.7. D495 2009
   658.4'092—dc22   2009017777

Printed in the United States of America
Designed by Carla Bolte · Set in Scala and Scala Sans

*To Raney, who looks to me for leadership,
and Susan, whose lead I'm happy to follow*

Contents

Leadership, Rulership, Stewardship, and Lemmingship

This is a book for people who aspire to be leaders or to understand leadership, so let's start with a simple definition: leaders strive to change the ways that other people think, feel, and act. Leadership is about creating change. While many people like to see themselves as leaders, mostly they are engaging in three different pursuits that we commonly confuse with leadership: rulership, stewardship, and lemmingship.

Rulership is about protecting and preserving one's position of power and privilege through methods that sometimes include manipulation, deception, coercion, force, and violence. Aspiring rulers have studied Niccolò Machiavelli's *The Prince* for centuries. In more recent times they've watched *The Godfather* film trilogy and *The Sopranos* television series.

Stewardship is the responsible and intelligent management of established institutions. Good stewards might run things much more efficiently and profitably than their predecessors did, but they don't try to change their culture's entrenched values and priorities. Stewardship is an admirable calling, and its practitioners have been well served for several decades by instructive authors ranging from Peter Drucker to Jim Collins.

Lemmingship occurs when the heads of organizations repeat the same practices and strategies that have already brought ruinous consequences for others in their fields (though they often get away with enriching themselves extraordinarily while they're at it). In recent decades America's automobile and airline industries have provided deplorable examples of lemmingship. And so has Wall Street, of course. Lemmingship is what we usually wind up with when leadership is what we really need.

This book isn't for aspiring rulers, stewards, or lemmings. It's about leaders and for leaders, and it sets out to explain the single most important thing that they need to do.

Leaders have only two tools at their disposal: what they say and how they act. What they say might be interesting, but how they act is always crucial. This book shows what happens in those unusual cases of true leaders who actually walk the walk.

Walk the Walk

Chapter One

When You Walk the Walk,
You Show What's Really Most Important

On September 28, 1962, Martin Luther King Jr. stood behind a podium in a crowded auditorium in Birmingham, Alabama. He was delivering the closing speech on the fourth and final day of the annual national gathering of the organization he headed, the Southern Christian Leadership Conference. Nearly all of the three hundred people in the audience that day were, like King himself, black Americans who were leaders in the civil rights movement. While their homes were scattered throughout the vast expanse of the South, and they represented seventy-five chapters of the organization, many of them knew each other from having attended other speeches and meetings and church services and protests and rallies and boycotts and marches. But sitting in the sixth row back from the stage was a twenty-four-year-old white man whom none of them had ever met. He sported bushy hair and wore a simple white T-shirt, which was conspicuously casual compared with the Sunday suits, pressed white shirts, and silk neckties that composed the unofficial uniform of King and his preacher colleagues. His name was Roy James, he lived in Arlington, Virginia, and the special agents of the Federal Bureau of Investigation knew him to be a member of the American Nazi Party. He was there in Birmingham on a mission. And listening to King's speech summoned the fury that he needed to carry it out despite the personal risk.

James leaped from his seat, vaulted onto the stage, and curled the fingers of his right hand into a fist. He punched King on the left cheek. The blow struck so hard and landed so cleanly that it made a loud noise. The historian Taylor Branch writes in *Parting the Waters* that King "staggered backward and spun half around" while "the entire crowd observed in silent, addled awe." But then the Nazi soldier pursued the black leader and struck him from behind on the side of the face. And then this assailant pounded his victim two times on the back. The audience shrieked. Roy James hit Martin Luther King Jr. again and again, knocking him farther back. At six feet two inches and two hundred pounds, tall and lean and powerful, the Nazi youth towered over the stocky five-foot-seven-inch preacher, who had already suffered bruises to his jaw, face, ear, and neck.

King finally managed to turn and face his assailant. And then King showed the stuff of truly great leadership: he dropped his hands and refused to fight back.

He was "turning the other cheek."

He was *walking the walk.*

Jesus said to turn the other cheek, and that's exactly what King, a Baptist minister, had been telling everyone in the civil rights movement for the previous six years, ever since 1956, when he got rid of his stash of guns even though his house had been bombed while his wife, Coretta, and their eldest child were inside. Whenever he stood at a podium and talked the talk, as he had that day, King preached that the way of "nonviolence" was the *only* way for their movement. And now, for the hundreds in that auditorium, who were leaders in their own right back home in their communities around the South, there could be no possible doubt that Martin Luther King believed it deeply. A man filled with hatred had struck him on the left cheek, and King turned the other cheek—had, indeed, intentionally left his whole person vulnerable to further injury.

Some of the delegates in the auditorium that day had been quietly critical of King for the hero worship he accepted from the media and from so many of his followers while they, the movement's many unsung heroes, still struggled in obscurity. But even they were profoundly moved as they watched King drop his hands and stand there defenseless in front of the attacker. One of those critics was Septima Clark, who was creating hundreds of remarkably effective "citizenship schools" for teaching illiterate, impoverished adults how to read and write and understand basic civics so they could register as responsible voters in the American democracy. Taylor Branch writes that even Septima Clark, who "would not have been shocked to see the unloosed rage of an exalted leader, marveled instead at King's transcendent calm. King dropped his hands 'like a newborn baby,' she said, and from then on she never doubted that nonviolence was more than the heat of his oratory or the result of his slow calculation. It was the response of his quickest instincts.

The impression struck a number of others, including perhaps the assailant himself." James stared at King, dumbstruck by King's extraordinary gesture.

In that brief moment some of the delegates came between the two men. James expected to be beaten by hundreds of black people acting in retaliation as a vicious mob.

"Don't touch him," King said. "Don't touch him. We have to pray for him."

And no one touched the attacker.

And they prayed for him instead.

King talked with James right there on the stage, reassuring him that no one would hurt him. Then King took James away from the crowd to a private room, and they talked peacefully. Even after James revealed that he was a Nazi, King refused to press charges.

That's the tremendous power of walking the walk. That's why Martin Luther King Jr. deserves his reputation as a great leader. The reason that those three hundred delegates that day in Birmingham, Alabama, overcame their instinctive reflexes and actually lived out the credo of nonviolence wasn't because King had given an inspiring speech extolling nonviolence. It was because they witnessed King himself turning the other cheek. The reason they had looked to him for leadership for six years wasn't because he was a superb orator. There were plenty of other terrific orators in the southern black churches. It was because he actually lived out his philosophy of nonviolence—and showed that it worked. It was because he directed a 381-day nonviolent boycott of the bus system in Montgomery, Alabama, and put an end to the city's practice of forcing blacks to give up seats to whites and move to the back of the bus. It was because his house and family had been bombed and he had been stabbed and shot at and beaten and arrested and imprisoned, and yet he never resorted to violence himself or advocated violence by his compatriots. By living by Jesus' teaching from the Sermon on the Mount, King proved to them that they, too, could live that way. That's why not one person among the three hundred in that auditorium moved to retaliate against the relentless Nazi attacker. That's why those leaders would leave Birmingham and go back to their cities and towns and hamlets throughout the South sustained in their belief and expectation that nonviolence would help them achieve equality in their time. That's why King was recognized as the leader of countless other gifted leaders who played historic roles, from Septima Clark, a granddaughter of slaves, who taught sharecroppers to become voters, to Rosa Parks, a seamstress, whose refusal to sit at the back of the bus instigated the Montgomery boycott. (The forty-nine-year-old Parks was there in the auditorium when King was assaulted by the Nazi, and afterward she administered her remedy of two aspirins and a Coca-Cola.)

As I write this book, forty-five years after King intoned "I Have a Dream" at the Lincoln Memorial in August 1963, it's still inspiring and moving to watch the video of that great speech and to hear the conviction in King's voice and to marvel at the prescience of his vision. There's no better example of talking the talk. But it's too bad we don't have a YouTube video of the 1962 assault by the Nazi, because that would show why people in his movement believed King when he said what was very hard for most people to believe, even though Jesus had said it, and why they joined King in doing what extraordinarily few people had done in the two thousand years since Jesus first suggested the unusual idea.

This story about Martin Luther King Jr. and Roy James helps illuminate many of the effects of walking the walk, but I've used it to begin chapter 1 because it shows one effect with particular sharpness. When you walk the walk, you reveal the ranking of your values. King's actions showed that nonviolence was his paramount value for the movement that he led. Although he sought many important things for black people in America— equality, respect, power, prosperity—he wouldn't sacrifice nonviolence to achieve any of them. Nonviolence was nonnegotiable. It was number one.

The most crucial role of a leader is establishing and instilling the one or two values that will be most important for an organization or a movement or a community. There are always a multitude of values that are well worth enshrining. The hard part is making the inevitable trade-offs between them: deciding *this* is more important than *that*. And the *hardest* part is showing that one particular thing, or two things, are the *most* important. John Rawls, a legendary political philosopher, called these "first virtues," and that's a term that I'll use in this book. I also like to call this the Rule of One or Two. For Martin Luther King Jr. I would list the first virtues, in order, like this:

No. 1: *nonviolence*
No. 2: *equality*

Put them together and you have "We will struggle nonviolently for equality." There was no doubt, then or now, that this was what King was all about. He was criticized by many people in his movement for his caution and slowness to assert leadership in other struggles, such as alleviating poverty and ending the war in Vietnam. And he did care passionately about both of those other causes. But King realized the necessity, and the power, of first virtues.

One thing that astonishes me about nearly every large publicly owned company that I've gotten to know is that they rarely clarify their first virtues even though they often waste a ridiculous amount of time, energy, and money trying to communicate their supposed values. Look at The Coca-Cola Company, for example: in 2004, when the board picked Neville Isdell as the third chief executive officer in five years, he brought together the troubled company's top 150 executives from around the world and asked them to start fresh and write a "manifesto" for change. The executives came up with a "vision" consisting of five goals, known as the "Five Ps": profit, people, planet, partners, and portfolio (meaning the company's collection of hundreds of brands). And the top 150 also produced a list of seven "shared *values* that we live by as a company and as individuals": leadership, passion, integrity, accountability, collaboration, innovation, and quality. They set forth these principles in a well-designed book and sent copies to tens of thousands of employees worldwide. Managers held special meetings to discuss the book in detail with their teams. Employees explored the meanings of the goals and values in online learning materials. The values were even proclaimed on a sign behind the front reception desk at the world headquarters. It must have seemed like a nearly perfect execution of what they teach at Harvard Business School about leadership for creating change: form a "guiding coalition" to set the "vision" and then "communicate, communicate, communicate."

In reality it was exasperating: how was anyone at Coca-Cola supposed to know how the organization's leaders would make the inescapable, hard trade-offs between its five goals? For example, which would be more important, "profit" or "people"? If profit trumped people, then the chief executive officer might feel justified about laying off thousands of loyal workers in order to achieve his lofty goal of double-digit earnings growth. But if people outweighed profit, then the CEO might settle for merely single-digit earnings growth, or even significant losses for a sustained length of time, to preserve the jobs of many faithful employees.

But the situation became even more absurd when you added the seven values to the five goals, resulting in a jumble of twelve elements; twelve undeniably good elements, for sure. But no one could possibly have any idea whether, when the time came for tough choices, *this* was more important than *that*, let alone which of the dozen considerations was *most* important. Was "integrity" more crucial than "profit," for instance? That question is constantly relevant for countless executives and employees in an

American company that operates in nearly every one of the world's nations, including many where bribery and corruption are the standard ways that business is done. Coca-Cola's people would get no useful guidance from how the top 150 "leaders" had talked the talk; but it didn't matter because what everyone soon watched was how the big boss walked the walk: Neville Isdell picked Muhtar Kent as his No. 2 executive in December 2006, and a year later, he named Kent as his successor. Those actions told everyone exactly what they needed to know.

Muhtar Kent had an intriguing history. In 1996, when he had been in charge of a Coca-Cola subsidiary that bottled the beverages in twelve overseas countries, he profited personally by betting that the subsidiary's stock price would fall. He sold the stock short: he borrowed a hundred thousand shares and immediately sold them to other investors. A few hours later, the company revealed some bad news that swiftly caused the stock price to sink by four dollars a share. Then Kent bought a hundred thousand shares at the reduced price and returned those shares to his lender. And so he had made a four-hundred-thousand-dollar profit in a few hours. This practice, called "short selling," is usually a dangerous gamble, but Kent's scheme had been entirely free of risk: his timing was perfect because as managing director of the bottling company he knew for certain that it was about to announce the disappointing news about earnings that would surely depress the share price. The fix was in.

What he did was blatantly illegal in just about any country that tries to regulate its stock market. Every executive of a publicly owned company knows such trading is unfair, illegal, and pernicious. You would have to be astonishingly ignorant to be the head of a public company and not know. But when Australia's stock-market regulators began investigating the transaction, Kent claimed that he didn't realize he did anything wrong. Either he was comically ignorant or he was blatantly lying. Either way, it looked awful that a Coca-Cola executive was profiting by betting against his stock rather than buying and holding the shares for many years to show the company's investors, employees, and partners his tremendous conviction in its long-term prospects. Kent was forced to return the illicit four-hundred-thousand-dollar profit plus fifty thousand dollars to cover the costs of the investigation, and he resigned from the bottling operation and went to work elsewhere. But four years later, Coca-Cola hired him back, and he resumed his rapid ascent through the company's ranks.

Surely it's generous to give a second chance to someone who made a big mistake. But any chief executive officer who truly valued "integrity" and "accountability" would never pick such a man as his president and chief operating officer, let alone as the next CEO of one of the largest and most influential corporations in all of global capitalism. And if Kent had shown "passion," it was for his personal profit rather than the good of his company. What an utter mockery of the "values" sign behind the reception desk! But Kent had a reputation for making money. Obviously, quarterly profit was still the "first virtue" of this corporation, despite the summit meeting of the top 150 "leaders" and all the time that everyone squandered talking the talk about *Our Manifesto for Growth*.

The Coca-Cola Company is shamefully typical of large corporations: its top executives devote an impressive amount of time, energy, and money to talking the talk about gallant goals and virtuous values, but ultimately they're driven by the first virtue of short-term profits. What's No. 1 to them isn't the planet, or their people, or their partners. Is there any doubt who's really No. 1 to the top executives of public corporations? Obviously, it's the stock analysts on Wall Street. Overwhelmingly, these companies are run in order to satisfy the demands of influential analysts. And the analysts are very clear about what they want. They're explicit about their first values. They have a perfect understanding of the Rule of One or Two. These are the things they crave, in order of importance:

No. 1: profit (short term)
No. 2: predictability

When you put those two together, the message is: "You will tell us in advance exactly how much to expect your quarterly profits to rise, and you *will* deliver on those expectations." When companies live by these first virtues—quarter after quarter, year after year—they are beloved by the Wall Street analysts, who reward them by talking up their stock prices. When they fail to "meet expectations," even for a single quarter, they imperil their relationship with the analysts. When they consistently "miss their numbers," they incur the wrath of the analysts and the countless investors who think the same way.

The alleged "leaders" of big companies may talk the talk with fervor. They may communicate, communicate, communicate a high-minded vision and a long list of uncontroversial values. They might even say that something or someone else is No. 1 to them rather than short-term profits or the Wall Street stock analysts. They might, for example, claim that "customers come first," or that "our people come first," or that "we run this company for the long term." But we all see how they walk the walk, and no one is fooled. Everyone knows that these CEOs practice lemmingship rather than leadership.

But let's stop for a minute and imagine this scenario: What if top executives were completely clear about their organizations' first virtues, and those virtues represented a real change from what nearly all of the business community had always practiced? And what if they actually walked the walk, and kept walking it? What if they actually put their customers first, or their employees first, or even their team of innovative thinkers first, rather than putting the Wall Street stock analysts first? Or if they really valued the long run (the next decade or two) more than the short term (the next three months)? Or if they actually enshrined one particular virtue—the reliability of their service, for example, or the cleanliness of their stores—far above any other possible vision or goal or value?

When such what-ifs have actually happened, we've seen real leaders. As I'll show in detail in the next two chapters, these practices have been crucial to the creation of some of the most remarkable successes in business history. They're behind the most successful airline of our times, the most successful Wall

Street investment bank, the most successful Internet retailer, the most successful consumer-electronics company, the most successful fast-food chain, and the most successful restaurant in the hypercompetitive restaurant market of New York City, among other great successes.

Chapter Two

When You Walk the Walk,
You Show Who Comes First

What if a public company actually put customers first? That's a real-life, large-scale, high-risk experiment we've seen conducted by Jeff Bezos ever since he founded the Internet retailer Amazon.com in 1994. From Amazon's early days, Bezos explained to everyone that his vision was "to create the world's most customer-centric company." He was also very clear that he was going to run the company for the long term. (He was thirty-one years old, and he wasn't planning on doing anything else anytime soon.) He practiced the Rule of One or Two. You could easily list his first virtues, in this order:

No. 1: customers
No. 2: long term

Of course, no company can sustain its business for the long run without making money. So, put No. 1 and No. 2 together and the message is that "we'll build a profitable, enduring company for the long run by putting customers first from the very beginning." This might sound conventional and clichéd, but when a leader actually puts it into practice, it's rare and revolutionary. Think of what it means. If you put customers first, what about the stock analysts and shareholders? What about executives and employees? What about business partners? All of those constituents might want to come first, but they won't. The customers will come first, and when they do, everyone else will feel overlooked, betrayed, bewildered, angry, or upset. They won't understand why you aren't serving *them*. Instead of hailing you as a visionary leader, they'll proclaim that you're stupid or incompetent or crazy, and they'll predict your downfall or they'll call for your ouster.

That's exactly what happened at Amazon. Early on, Bezos decided to enable customers to post their own reviews of the products that Amazon was trying to sell, including negative reviews—*extremely* negative reviews. Many observers were befuddled by the move. As Bezos told me in an interview for a cover story I wrote about him in *Fast Company*: "I started receiving letters from well-meaning folks, saying: 'Perhaps you don't understand your business? You make money when you sell things. Why are you allowing negative reviews on your website?'" What's more, many of Bezos's business partners—the creators and publishers of the books, movies, and music that Amazon sold—were outraged. But Bezos stuck with the move because it fit perfectly with the Rule of One or Two. No. 1: It was good for their customers, he felt, since reading reviews by other customers helped them make better decisions about what to buy. And No. 2: He believed it would be good for Amazon in the long run, because those customers might ultimately buy more stuff from Amazon if they found from experience that the Web site did everything possible to be useful to them and to serve their interest. And giving customers a voice on the Web site made them feel like valued participants in a community of their peers rather than targets of a company interested only in their money.

That was just the beginning. Since then, Bezos has introduced many other innovations that have measurably hurt Amazon's sales and profits, at least in the short run, but they were always driven by his belief that what's good for the customer would ultimately turn out to be in the company's enlightened self-interest.

For example, Bezos decided to let third parties compete with Amazon by selling products on what he calls the Web site's "prime real estate": the product details page. This means that customers can see listings from a number of rival companies— and many small-timers, including Amazon's own customers— offering the same digital camera side by side with the one Amazon sells, but perhaps at a lower price, or a used copy of a book that Amazon sells new. "The decision was very controversial within the company," Bezos told me. "There was a lot of anxiety around it." Once again, Bezos acted from his inherent faith in giving greater choice to customers.

"Sometimes we measure things and see that in the short term they actually hurt sales, and we do it anyway," Bezos said, because he doesn't think the short term is a good predictor of the long term. His managers found that their biggest customers had such large collections of stuff—especially CDs—that they accidentally ordered items they had already bought from Amazon years ago. So they decided to give people a warning whenever this was about to happen. Sure enough, the warnings reduced Amazon's sales in the short run. But it was hard to predict the feature's long-term effects. Would it reduce sales over a ten-year period? They didn't think so. They thought it would make customers happy and probably increase sales. Bezos said, "In cases like that, we say, 'Let's be simpleminded. We know this is a feature that's good for customers. Let's do it.'"

Amazon faced similar dilemmas with its dramatic moves to cut prices and offer free shipping on orders of twenty-five dollars or more, which were very costly to the company. "You can do the math fifteen different ways, and every time the math tells you that you shouldn't lower prices because you're gonna make less money," Bezos says. "That's undoubtedly true in the current quarter, in the current year. But it's probably not true over a ten-year period, when the benefit is going to increase the frequency with which your customers shop with you, the fraction of purchases they do with you as opposed to other places. Their overall satisfaction is going to go up." Later Bezos introduced Amazon Prime, which offers unlimited second-day shipping for a flat fee of seventy dollars a year, even though many hard-core customers (such as myself) wouldn't have flinched about spending hundreds of dollars a year more for shipping. Amazon Prime meant leaving a big pile of money on the table.

Now that Amazon is midway through its second decade, Bezos has been proven correct. He has recruited tens of millions of extremely loyal customers. In the University of Michigan's annual survey of customers' satisfaction with two hundred major American corporations, Amazon usually ranks at or near the very top. In the study conducted at the end of 2007, Amazon eclipsed every other company with a score of 88, beating out well-loved brand names such as Lexus (the leader among car companies, at 87), Nordstrom (the top bricks-and-mortar retailer, at 80) and Southwest Airlines (No. 1 among airlines, at 76). Amazon's "golden reputation," in the words of the *New York Times*, is especially astonishing considering that it came during a period of incredibly rapid growth.

While Bezos was gaining the appreciation and loyalty of customers, he spent many years weathering the hatred of Wall Street stock analysts, who wanted predictable profits *now*, not the promise of a giant, profitable, enduring company to come sometime *later*. The *New York Times* wrote: "From the first shareholder letter he wrote back in 1997, he has consistently made clear that he would run Amazon by focusing on the future and shrugging off short-term worries. He said he would 'relentlessly slash prices,' even if it cut into incremental profits, because he was convinced that it was the right thing to do." And so, year after year, Amazon lost money. Lots of money. Billions and billions of dollars, seemingly lost forever. Every quarter, when news reporters called the Wall Street analysts for comments about Amazon's results, they complained about the company's inexcusably low margins and lambasted Bezos for leaving all that money on the table. By 2000, the analysts were calling for Amazon's board of directors to remove Bezos from power. They claimed that Bezos didn't have any idea how to run a corporation.

The reality was that Bezos was running a corporation as a real leader. He was doing it his way, not their way. He was challenging the deep-rooted ways that investors thought, felt, and acted. Amazon finally reported a small profit in 2003, seven years after going public, but Bezos was still brazenly unconcerned about serving the stock analysts: as the company was turning ten years old in 2004, Amazon had failed to live up to the analysts' expectations for its earnings in three out of four consecutive quarters.

But Bezos wouldn't put Wall Street first. Nor would he put his employees first by sacrificing other values in order to preserve their jobs. At one point, after Amazon expanded too rapidly, Bezos laid off one-seventh of its workforce, a serious blow to employees' morale and loyalty. But Bezos accepted having to alienate analysts, employees, executives, and partners because his Rule of One or Two was all about customers. And ultimately that "golden reputation" is what enabled Amazon to become a giant, profitable, enduring company that survived global economic downturns, hired thousands of additional employees, enriched countless senior executives, and ultimately won over many of the business partners who had castigated it in the earlier days. As of late 2008, Amazon had more than eighteen thousand employees, and its stock market value was $31 billion, higher than any other company that sells physical goods over the Internet, even eBay. Amazon was actually an expensive stock: its price-earnings ratio was 54 compared with the average of 31 for the Standard & Poor's index of five hundred major companies. These figures underscore the fact that a large num-

ber of investors ignored the conventional, myopic way of thinking and entrusted their money to Bezos for the longer run.

"With respect to investors, there's a great Warren Buffettism,"
Bezos once told me. "You can hold a rock concert and that can
be successful, and you can hold a ballet and that can be successful, but don't hold a rock concert and advertise it as a ballet. If
you're very clear to the outside world that you're taking a long-
term approach, then people can self-select in. You get shareholders who want you to relentlessly lower prices. As Buffett says, you
get the shareholders you deserve." Jeff Bezos has certainly been
clear about his long-term approach, and the source of that clarity
is how he's walked the walk and kept walking it. If he had just
talked glowingly about creating the "world's most customer-
centric company," no one would have believed him. He would
have sounded very much like thousands of dot-com-era entrepreneurs who did nothing more than talk the talk. It was only by
sticking with decision after decision that benefited customers
while angering and bewildering everyone else that Jeff Bezos
proved he's the real thing.

In 2005 Cable News Network (CNN) convened a panel of experts
to rank the twenty-five most influential business leaders of the
previous twenty-five years. In 2007 *USA Today* asked the reporters and editors of its Money section to do the same thing, and
they asked for their readers' opinions through a poll. Jeff Bezos
appeared on all three of these rankings of the top twenty-five of
the past twenty-five years, and deservedly so. But Bezos still has
to walk the walk for many more years before he can hope to

match the extraordinary achievements of a business leader who preceded him, a man whose name—Sidney James Weinberg—is no longer well known. Weinberg ran Goldman Sachs from 1930 until his death, at age seventy-seven, in 1969, transforming the company from a sleepy also-ran into the preeminent investment bank on Wall Street. It has held that enviably prestigious and lucrative position for several decades and maintained its exceptional corporate culture long after Weinberg was gone.

Weinberg's leadership secret was simple: he intuitively understood the power of the Rule of One or Two, and he practiced the same first virtues as Bezos did:

> **No. 1: *customers (known in his world as "clients")***
> **No. 2: *long term***

Lisa Endlich describes these clear priorities in *Goldman Sachs: The Culture of Success*, her well-researched history of the company: "Goldman Sachs believed in and observed the religion of client service, and its focus remained steadfastly on the long term. Simple as it sounds, the firm's success can be traced to its iron grip on those two values."

To be sure, nearly everyone on Wall Street has always talked the talk about putting clients first and nurturing client relationships for the long term—and then they've always worked fiercely for the highest possible short-term profits for their firms, which in turn produced enviable year-end bonuses for themselves. Weinberg actually put clients first, and he did so for twenty-five years before his prodigious efforts began bringing in lucrative profits to his own company. Ultimately, though, that quarter-century of walking the walk led to a half century in which Goldman Sachs was the top institution on Wall Street.

Weinberg's story is astonishing. Growing up as one of eleven children of a poor family in Brooklyn's Red Hook—which, even a century later, remained a hardscrabble neighborhood—he dropped out of the eighth grade to work full-time. In 1907, at age fifteen, he rode the elevator to the top of the twenty-five-story Wall Street tower that was the tallest skyscraper in New York City at the time. Starting there at the top, he asked for a job on every floor, making his way down. He was rejected twenty-three times before he had descended all the way to the second floor, where Goldman Sachs hired him for three dollars a week as an assistant to the janitor and porter. He cleaned spittoons, shined shoes, and filled inkwells. And the company's patriarchs, Henry Goldman and Samuel Sachs, called him "boy."

Sidney Weinberg ultimately became the head of the firm in 1930, at age thirty-eight. Wall Street had just been devastated by the stock-market crash of October 1929, so there was little profit to be made, especially at a place like the Goldman Sachs of that era. The firm that Weinberg took over was a very small player in the financial markets, and it would remain so for a long time. "The firm's combined profits from 1930 to 1945 were zero," Endlich reports. For the years 1938 to 1947, Goldman Sachs ranked twelfth in market share for firms that sold new issues of stocks and bonds to the public. With a 1.4 percent share, it did only about one-tenth as much business as the handful of houses that really ran Wall Street, which included Morgan Stanley (at 16 percent) and First Boston (at 13 percent).

But all through the '30s and '40s, Weinberg was doing something remarkable. He developed a reputation for selfless devotion to the needs and interests of the people who ran America's top corporations. He cultivated close personal friendships with them and slowly earned their trust by giving them consistently good advice over many years—even though they either weren't clients of Goldman Sachs (not yet, at least) or their companies gave very little business to the firm. One example of Weinberg's extreme service was how he participated on corporate boards of directors. Board members were (and still are) notorious for simply showing up at meetings and rubber-stamping the plans of the chief executive officers. But Weinberg tapped the energies of Goldman Sachs's younger staffers to help him prepare thoroughly for the meetings so he could offer valuable insights. "To Weinberg, to serve on corporate boards was almost a religion," Endlich writes. Weinberg's energies became appreciated by the heads of companies such as General Electric, who realized that an expert's advice was more useful than a rubber stamp. They came to rely on him. He served on more than thirty boards, attending 250 meetings a year of the full boards or his board committees. And he prepared carefully for all of them.

Weinberg became a highly respected figure among the corporate elite and was known as "the Director's Director" and "Mr. Wall Street." But his selfless service hadn't paid off yet for Goldman Sachs. As the 1950s began, the firm didn't even rank in Wall Street's top seventeen in market share. Weinberg's breakthrough came a few years later, and it sprang from a friendship he cultivated for nearly a decade without seeking profit for himself or his firm. In 1947 Weinberg had met Henry Ford II, who had recently taken over his family business, the Ford Motor Company, which was America's biggest corporation at the time. "Ford began to look to him for business advice," Endlich writes. "The relationship became so close that Ford later described Weinberg as his best friend." It was an ironic twist of history considering that the first Henry Ford was notoriously anti-Semitic.

For years, the former shoeshine boy advised the scion of the American dynasty, coming up with fifty different plans for revamping the finances of Ford Motor Company. But "there was never a formal agreement, a contract, or any discussion of the fees Goldman Sachs would charge for the services he offered." In 1956, after Sidney Weinberg had spent nine years giving free advice and putting his close friend's interests and needs far above his own, Henry Ford II chose Goldman Sachs as the lead manager for the $650 million worth of stock that it planned to sell to the public—the biggest sale of stock to the public *ever.* Goldman Sachs became Ford Motor's sole investment banker, profiting greatly from the account. And that single deal launched Goldman's swift ascent into the top ranks of Wall Street firms. In 1958 Goldman Sachs was hired by Sears, Roebuck, the retailing giant, to handle the biggest bond sale in U.S. history. That year, *Time* magazine acknowledged the new king of finance by writing, "The Wall Streeter whose advice is most often sought by U.S. businessmen is Sidney J. Weinberg."

Goldman Sachs reigned as the top house on Wall Street for a half century to follow. And its success sprang from Sidney

Weinberg's great leadership. From 1930 to 1956, a long period in which his company remained a minor player, he had faithfully followed the Rule of One or Two, walking the walk of putting clients first and nurturing relationships for the long term, placing those first virtues far above short-term profit for himself or his firm. "Weinberg's highest priority was establishing a top investment bank with a first-rate client list—not making money for himself or Goldman Sachs," Endlich writes. "Above all, he showed unswerving devotion to his clients. . . . For decades to come Goldman Sachs would benefit from the goodwill generated by this one man."

Instead of putting customers first, as both Bezos and Weinberg did, what if a leader put *employees* first? That's an equally revolutionary idea. And it's the first virtue behind the unprecedented success of Southwest Airlines, which *Fortune* magazine called "the most successful airline in history."

Ever since turning its first profit in 1973, as a six-year-old start-up, Southwest has been profitable every year for thirty-five years. Meanwhile, most other major airlines were rarely profitable for more than three or four years at a stretch. In late 2008 Southwest ranked first among U.S. airlines with a stock-market valuation of $11 billion. That was more than $8 billion higher than the No. 2 and more than the combined values of the next four competitors (American, Delta, Northwest, and Continental). While its low fares make Southwest only the sixth biggest airline in terms of revenues, it is the richest, the most profitable, the most valuable, and it carries more passengers (104 million a year) than any other airline in the world.

In July 2008 Southwest reported a quarterly profit—its sixty-ninth straight quarter of profitability (meaning more than seventeen years' worth). Meanwhile, the six other major airlines all announced huge quarterly losses, totaling $6 billion, and laid off thousands of employees. The others blamed their losses and lay-offs on jet fuel prices, which had doubled in the past year and reached a record high. But Southwest Airlines didn't lay off any-one. Southwest had never laid off any employees—not when fuel prices broke records, and not even when it was losing millions of dollars a day in the weeks following the terrorist attacks of September 11, 2001, when planes were grounded and the other airlines reacted by collectively laying off more than a hundred thousand people.

The pair of leaders responsible for the greatness of Southwest Airlines—Herb Kelleher, the chief executive officer, and Colleen Barrett, the president—grasped the Rule of One or Two and were clear about their first virtues:

No. 1: employees
No. 2: profitability

In their long and spectacular run together as a team, Kelleher and Barrett made everyone understand that No. 1 came before No. 2: Southwest needed to be profitable—and, for that matter, to have a strong financial position (keeping billions of dollars of cash on hand and avoiding taking on much debt)—so it could get through hard times without layoffs. This enlightened thinking represented a revolutionary approach for the airline industry, which has suffered from lemmingship as bad as any sector of American capitalism.

The lemming who led the way was a man named Frank Lorenzo, who took over Continental Airlines in 1981. Lorenzo had the airline file for bankruptcy. That gave him the legal right to cancel Continental's contracts with its labor unions, which he did. He fired all the unionized employees and hired a new workforce at salaries only half as high. He cut their benefits, too, and forced them to work longer hours and take shorter breaks. As a result Continental's costs fell dramatically, and it made a profit for three years in a row. In the meantime Lorenzo borrowed billions of dollars to take over a bunch of other carriers—including Eastern Airlines, Frontier Airlines, People Express, and New York Air—and assemble the largest airline company in America.

But Lorenzo's strategy was disastrous for everyone— employees, customers, shareholders—other than himself. He had an awful relationship with the employees he paid so poorly. Their morale was terrible: "When you went to work for Frank Lorenzo, there was no compassion," explained Carla Winkler, a flight attendant. "The employees, they were a commodity, like a file cabinet, like a desk, or a chair. They just moved the pieces around, and you weren't to have any feelings." Working in this disheartening atmosphere, Continental's employees lost more baggage, clocked more late departures, and received more complaints than any other airline. And Lorenzo struggled to pay the interest on the massive debt he had taken on to have the bragging rights of being the biggest airline company. In 1990, he sold the business. The situation was so bad that Continental was forced into bankruptcy for the second time in less than a decade, and Eastern—which was once a great airline—went out of business. But other executives had to notice that Frank Lorenzo himself walked away with $30 million in personal profit.

Nearly every major airline CEO has followed the infamous example of Frank Lorenzo. It's one of the most deplorable cases of lemmingship in American business. When times were good they would borrow heavily to expand, and then, when times turned bad, they would quickly lose billions of dollars on top of the billions they couldn't afford to repay creditors. They would file for bankruptcy as a way of laying off thousands of employees, drastically cutting salaries and benefits, reneging on pensions, and putting off or shortchanging creditors. And the CEOs would pay themselves tens of millions of dollars for spending a few years presiding over these disasters. Nearly all of Southwest's rivals have followed this model. Nearly all of the major airlines have declared bankruptcy: US Airways and United in 2002, Air Canada in 2003, Aloha in 2004, Northwest and Delta in 2005. The dubious exception is American Airlines, which threatened to file for bankruptcy in 2003 in order to force its unions to accept pay cuts.

The lemmingship of the big airlines is inexcusable, especially since Herb Kelleher and Colleen Barrett showed a better alternative—and real leadership—at Southwest. When they were talking the talk, they created a list of eleven "primary attitudes" for the airline. Eleven is, in my view, far too many, but they were very clear about which came first: "Employees are number one. The way you treat your employees is the way they will treat your customers." And that's how they actually walked the walk for three decades. The biggest way their actions proved it was that they never laid off employees, not even when the economy was troubled. As Southwest's people watched Frank Lorenzo and other airline CEOs "furlough" thousands, Kelleher never furloughed anyone. When they saw other airlines file for bankruptcy, Southwest made money every year and spread the wealth around through profit sharing with employees. When Kelleher profited from his stock options, large numbers of Southwest rank-and-file workers did the same thing.

"Nothing kills your company's culture like layoffs," Kelleher said. "Nobody has ever been furloughed, and that is unprecedented in the airline industry. It's been a huge strength of ours. It's certainly helped us negotiate our union contracts. One of the union leaders—a Teamsters leader—came in to negotiate one time and he said, 'We know we don't need to talk with you about job security.' We could have furloughed at various times and been more profitable, but I always thought that was shortsighted. You want to show your people that you value them and you're not going to hurt them just to get a little more money in the short term. Not furloughing people breeds loyalty. It breeds a sense of security. It breeds a sense of trust." Sure enough, when Kelleher retired as chairman in 2008, at age seventy-seven, the pilots' union took out a full-page ad in *USA Today* thanking him and saying that "it has been an honor and a privilege to be part of his aviation legacy."

Because Kelleher and Barrett practiced the Rule of One or Two, they passed over other values and goals that distracted their rivals. Perhaps most important they weren't lured by trying to be one of the biggest airlines in terms of annual revenues, which is how size is usually measured in their business. Southwest took three times longer to reach $1 billion in revenues as did America West, which followed Lorenzo's example in the early 1990s and bought up a bunch of smaller carriers, taking on a crippling $2 billion of debt. While bragging rights about size didn't tempt Kelleher and Barrett to expand recklessly, neither did they seek the prestige of flying the most glamorous routes or the newest, biggest, or fanciest airplanes. "We don't care whether we fly to Paris," Kelleher said. (They made good money flying between smaller domestic cities such as Amarillo, Texas, and Tulsa, Oklahoma.) "We don't care whether we have a 747," he said. (By flying only a single type of plane, the smaller Boeing 737, Southwest's employees were able to become so familiar with that one model that they became much more efficient at flying it.) "What we're focused on is being profitable and job-secure," Kelleher added.

And that's exactly what they did. And after doing it year after year, Southwest's employees grasped that Kelleher really meant it. They knew that Southwest wanted them there for long careers and wouldn't lay them off once they gained seniority and started earning high salaries and benefits and securing pensions they could retire on. They knew that Kelleher and Barrett would never wage war against the unions that represented Southwest's pilots, flight attendants, mechanics and maintenance technicians, customer service and reservations agents, ramp and operations agents, and flight dispatchers. And that was crucial to getting people to embrace and master the many innovative practices that Southwest introduced. Countless articles and entire books have been written about Southwest's unique approach—how they got pilots and mechanics and ramp agents to cooperate so well and be able to turn around planes quickly at the gate and work more productively than anyone else in the business, which was Southwest's key to cutting costs. But all of that innovation was possible only because of the goodwill from walking the walk and putting employees first—even above profitability, even in difficult times.

As I write this book in 2008, it's astonishing that the other six major airlines have been losing billions of dollars while Southwest keeps making money. The key to Southwest's profits this year have been the way it locked in jet fuel supplies in advance at reasonable rates to protect against price increases, so when fuel prices shot up to record highs, Southwest could still make money. Now you don't need to be a financial genius to come up with this kind of so-called hedging strategy. It's something that any freshman economics student at any respectable university would surely understand. It's a common tactic in many other industries that are vulnerable to sudden surges in commodity prices.

And so why couldn't the very highly paid CEOs of American,

Delta, Northwest, US Airways, and United grasp the concept of locking in fuel prices, especially since the United States was waging a major war near some of the world's biggest oil fields, a factor that could easily disrupt supply? The only logical answer that I can come up with is that the other airline CEOs weren't really interested in profits during an economic slump. They rely on market downturns as a chance to undermine unions, cut costs, and put off creditors through the legal weapon of bankruptcy. That's the way they've run things for a long while. In their Rule of One or Two, the first virtues are harsh cost-cutting (in bad times) and overexpansion (in good times), even though this has created an industry that's loathed by employees and customers. At least there's one leader among the lemmings.

Like Herb Kelleher and Colleen Barrett in the airline industry, other leaders scattered throughout assorted businesses have put employees first—and that first virtue has been crucial to how they've ascended to the top of their fields and earned unmatched reputations with customers. One example is Danny Meyer, the most successful restaurateur in New York City, one of the most brutally competitive restaurant markets in the world. In his early years of running his first restaurant, the Union Square Cafe, Meyer (then in his twenties) resolved that "we must care for our own staff first." That first virtue inspired Meyer to ban smoking from his restaurant's dining room in 1990 and then from its bar area as well in 1991. Meyer was caring for the health of his servers, bartenders, cooks, and bus staff, even though the move risked alienating, or losing, much of the restaurant's clientele. "Some people thought I was crazy," Meyer recalls in his memoir, *Setting the Table.*

One customer who objected was Roger Straus, the cofounder and publisher of Farrar, Straus & Giroux, arguably the most prestigious book publisher in America. Straus's office was around the corner, and he lunched at the Union Square Cafe every day. More than any other "regular," Straus's familiar presence had helped establish and sustain the restaurant's following among the literary and creative people in the neighborhood. Would Danny Meyer risk losing his *best* customer, who came every day, year after year, in order to protect the health of workers in a business with notoriously high turnover?

He did. And it turned out that the Union Square Cafe's business *improved.* Its popularity continued to grow. Roger Straus kept coming back for lunch every day—and, ultimately, he gave up smoking completely. In 1995, four years after Meyer took a daring risk with his own smoking ban, New York City prohibited smoking in restaurant dining rooms. But the new law left some big loopholes: it allowed smokers in restaurant's bars, outdoor smoking sections, and small establishments with thirty-five seats or fewer. These exemptions appeared to give a crucial advantage to restaurants that still welcomed smokers and gave them a place to light up and puff away. But two years later, the completely smoke-free Union Square Cafe was named the most popular restaurant in New York City by the Zagat survey of tens of thousands of customers. It was only the fourth restaurant in the seventeen-year history of the influential poll to capture the

No. 1 ranking. And the Union Square Cafe held the "most popular" title for six straight years until 2003, when the city finally banned smoking completely in all restaurants, bars, and nightclubs. That year, the title of most popular restaurant was claimed by Gramercy Tavern, the *second* restaurant started by Danny Meyer, which he had kept smoke-free from the start. And the two places have swapped the title back and forth up through this writing in 2008.

To be sure, many other important factors enabled Meyer to become the preeminent restaurateur in New York City, and I'll discuss different aspects of his leadership at various points later in this book. But there's no doubt that his extraordinary results spring from practicing first virtues and the Rule of One or Two. By truly putting employees first, Meyer was able to recruit, train, and retain a staff that delivered superb service and distinguished his restaurants among the countless rivals in the city. His remarkable success comes from being a true leader—someone who challenges and changes the deep-rooted ways that we think, feel, and act—rather than a lemming.

Herb Kelleher and Colleen Barrett put employees first at Southwest Airlines, and Danny Meyer put employees first at the Union Square Cafe, but Masaru Ibuka, the founder of Sony, went even further from the usual way of running companies: he set out to put a very *particular* group of his employees above all others. Ibuka was an engineer, and he wanted to create a company dedicated to people just like him: brilliant engineers whose greatest satisfaction and highest sense of purpose came from overcoming especially difficult technological challenges through their creativity, resourcefulness, and originality. That's how he "talked the talk" when he wrote a ten-page "Founding Prospectus" for his company in Tokyo in 1946. Ibuka set forth eight "purposes of incorporation," and the first and overriding objective was "creating an ideal workplace, free, dynamic, and joyous, where dedicated engineers will be able to realize their craft and skill at the highest possible level." That first purpose didn't mention shareholders, or even customers; the company *existed* for its engineers. Ibuka also set forth a number of "management principles" for Sony, and the first and foremost among them was "we shall eliminate any untoward profit-seeking, shall constantly emphasize activities of real substance . . ."

Ibuka's prospectus is an amazing document, but what's even more extraordinary is how he "walked the walk" for the following three decades. He actually ran the company as a place where no value was higher than engineers fulfilling what they saw as their calling. And the greatest proof came in the 1960s, when Sony had to make vexing choices as it was struggling to develop a breakthrough technology for color television.

To understand this great test of Ibuka's first virtue, his Rule of One or Two, we have to look back to the early days of color TV. In 1964, only 3.1 percent of American households had color TV. Although the technology had been available for more than a decade, the quality of the pictures remained disappointing. The costs of the sets were still much too high. The viewers were satisfied with their black-and-white sets. And the networks broadcast few shows in color. NBC offered the most color programming only because its parent company, RCA, was the No. 1 manufacturer of color TV sets.

But color TV was nearing its breakthrough. A study in March 1965 predicted that NBC would attract more viewers than ABC or CBS because of its color programming. That study inspired all three networks to rush to convert their full schedules to color. It was clear to everyone in the business that color was about to explode in popularity at last.

By that time Sony's engineers had already spent four years trying to design a better TV set, but they hadn't improved on RCA's technology. As they kept toiling, Sony's rivals profited from the sudden surge in color TV sales. Sales of color TV sets in the United States, the wealthiest and most promising market, rose from 1.5 million in 1964 to 5.2 million in 1966. Sony could have rushed to make an imitative product and put it into this booming marketplace as an easy way of cashing in on the trend. It would have been a safe strategy for quick sales and profits. It was the path that nearly all of Japan's consumer electronics companies had pursued in the decades of revitalizing its economy following World War II. But that wasn't why Ibuka had founded Sony when the war had ended, and now, a full two decades later, it still wasn't how he actually ran the company.

"The potential market was huge," writes John Nathan in *Sony: The Private Life*, but Ibuka refused to copy: "His insistence on originality no matter what the cost seems to have been genuine, at the heart of his vision for himself and the company."

By autumn 1966, Nathan writes, Sony was "close to ruin" from its fruitless investment in research and its long failure to enter the market, but Ibuka still wouldn't compromise his first principles: he decided that Sony would "continue looking for a distinctive Sony solution. The engineers involved were unwilling to allow five years of work [to] end with imitation: Sony had been founded by Ibuka precisely in order to be a company for engineers."

Eventually, a twenty-nine-year-old member of the engineering team came up with a promising idea and developed it into a breakthrough technology—a significant improvement in picture quality. He brilliantly overcame the vexing problems of distorted images and distracting glare. Sony called the new product the "Trinitron," and Ibuka openly cried when he watched the first of the new TV sets being finished at the factory.

Sony was very late to market when it first sold the Trinitron in 1968. The portion of American households that already owned color TVs had already surged from 3 percent to 24 percent, and other brands had gotten a crucial head start. But customers realized that the Trinitron was a superior product, and they made it a phenomenal success. The Trinitron became the No. 1 selling TV set and remained the top model for decades. Sony sold 180 million Trinitrons between 1968 and 1988. It holds the title of best-selling TV *ever*. In 1992, when *Fortune* interviewed the eighty-three-year-old Ibuka and asked him "What's your favorite Sony product?" he said it was the Trinitron "because we bet the company" on that technology "and in twenty-three years nobody else has been able to match it." In 1997, when Ibuka died at eighty-nine, the *New York Times* praised him for how "Sony helped establish Japan's reputation for innovation by defying a tradition of copying products of others." And it said that Ibuka's leadership of the Trinitron project helped to make Sony "one of the most admired and competitive consumer products companies in the world."

Chapter Three

When You Walk the Walk,
You Show What Comes First

So far we've examined business leaders who have created the most successful companies in their fields by putting *someone* first—customers or employees or even engineers. Now let's see what happens when a leader puts *something* first, when they enshrine one principle as their first virtue rather than the interests of a particular group of people.

This approach is just as powerful. It has enabled a number of leaders to create revolutions in their industries. Let's take a quick look at three examples: Ray Kroc at McDonald's, Fred Smith at FedEx, and Charles Schwab at the company that carries his own name.

In the early years of McDonald's in the 1950s, Ray Kroc "talked the talk" of holding up three things as most important: quality, service, and cleanliness. These became known as "QSC," an acronym that's still widely used in the fast-food business today. Some years later Kroc added a *V* for value. While all four of these virtues are important for fast-food restaurants, no one ever escapes the Rule of One or Two: Kroc's repeated actions, rather than his stated credo, showed which of the four things he felt was the *most* important. From the way that Kroc walked the walk, everyone at McDonald's saw clearly that his greatest passion—his magnificent obsession—was cleanliness.

While Kroc was trying to recruit people to buy and run McDonald's franchises around the country in the 1950s, he personally owned and ran the McDonald's in the Chicago suburb of Des Plaines, Illinois. At this model site, he showed through his personal example the constant vigilance about cleanliness that he expected for everyone else: "Every night, you'd see him coming down the street, walking close to the gutter, picking up every McDonald's wrapper and cup along the way," recalled Fred Turner, who worked the grill at the restaurant. "He'd come into the store with both hands full of cups and wrappers. He was the store's outside pickup man." Kroc himself hosed down the parking lot, emptied the trash cans, and used a putty knife to scrape gum off the concrete outside. Turner was deeply impressed by his boss's obsessiveness: "I saw Ray spend one Saturday morning with a toothbrush cleaning out the holes in the mop wringer," Turner recalled. "No one else really paid any attention to the damned mop ringer, because everyone knew it was *just* a mop bucket. But Kroc saw all the crud building up in the holes, and he wanted to clean them so the wringer would work better."

Perfectionistic cleanliness was the first virtue that made it possible for McDonald's to achieve its other virtues. When people first heard about McDonald's, they had to overcome a natural skepticism that a restaurant offering such a superb value—it sold hamburgers for only fifteen cents—could offer a quality product. The design of the facilities helped overcome that resistance: they were brightly lit and had kitchens enclosed by glass so customers could see for themselves that all the fresh-looking ingredients were being prepared under the most wholesome conditions. Cleanliness made it much easier to convince people about quality and value. When Fred Turner first saw McDonald's, he thought: "It was so clean, so bright, so colorful. It was demonstration cooking. All the food preparation was out in the open. There was all that glistening stainless steel. And the uniforms of the crew were white and clean." The pervasive cleanliness proved to be a big draw for parents looking for a place to take their children, playing into Kroc's strategy of popularizing a place for families. (Previously, drive-ins had been patronized by raucous teenagers, whose presence drove away everyone else.)

Fred Turner became Ray Kroc's protégé and quickly rose from grill man to executive. In 1958 he produced a seventy-five-page manual, printed and bound, about how to run McDonald's franchises—and half of the manual was about detailed procedures for cleaning, which showed everyone that without doubt cleanliness was Kroc's highest value. John F. Love writes in his book *McDonald's: Behind the Arches* that *"every day* the windows had to be cleansed, the lot hosed down, and the garbage and waste cans scrubbed. Every other day, all stainless steel in the store, including such typically ignored areas as exhaust stacks, had to be polished. Every week, the ceiling of the store had to be washed. Mopping floors and wiping counters became a continuous process, and the cleaning cloth became an essential tool for every crew member. 'If you've got time to lean, you've got time to clean' was perhaps the first Krocism that influenced the entire system and shaped its operating philosophy." But if Ray Kroc had simply handed out a detailed seventy-five-page manual asking them to do far more than anyone had ever done, his will would have been thwarted by skepticism, apathy, resistance, and disobedience. The way he walked the walk—visibly, constantly, and passionately—made a terrific difference.

Ray Kroc's vision is still proving to have been astonishingly farsighted. A 2003 study by University of Wisconsin professors Martin S. Meyers and Scott Wallace found that cleanliness was the No. 1 factor for customers in choosing a fast-food restaurant, more important than convenient location, parking, price, taste, nutritional value, menu variety, atmosphere, employee friendliness and competence, employee compensation, speed of service, or in-store promotions. But what's most instructive about Kroc's leadership isn't that he realized the lasting importance of cleanliness. It's that he actually got tens of thousands of employees to keep thousands of restaurants immaculately clean. He was a great business leader not because of what he said, but what he actually did.

Under the leadership of Fred Smith, its founder and chairman, the FedEx company "talked the talk" by creating one of America's most famous advertising campaigns. Beginning in the 1970s, the ads assured customers that FedEx would "absolutely, positively," get their packages delivered to the right destinations on the next day. Fred Smith followed the Rule of One or Two: he enshrined *reliability* as the company's first virtue. That meant that FedEx needed to be run in an utterly different way than almost every major American corporation had been run up to that time. FedEx's employees, especially the ones scattered out in the field, needed to learn how to think quickly and take action, without waiting for direction or approval from their higher-ups, in order to solve the unexpected problems that other companies would surely accept as excuses for not getting things done. That was the culture that Smith had to create and nurture, and the only way to do it was for him and his executives to begin by setting a personal example.

Fred Smith's passion for reliability is legendary among FedEx's people, who like to tell the story about the executive who once made the mistake of arriving a few minutes late for an early-morning meeting with Smith and some other people at headquarters. The latecomer tried to excuse himself by explaining that the road he was taking to the office had been blocked by a freight train passing through. His excuse was received with a long, uncomfortable silence, and then Fred Smith asked, "Why didn't you have a Plan B?"

Throughout the company, from the managers in Memphis to the couriers driving trucks and delivering packages around the country, employees learned the art of Plan B: how to improvise, adapt, and overcome obstacles in order to get the job done on time. When Steven Schott's FedEx truck broke down in the middle of his route in Boulder, Colorado, he borrowed a bicycle from a customer, strapped packages to his back, and rode ten miles up and down steep hills in ninety-degree heat to finish his deliveries. When Larry Giammarino found that for some mysterious reason the combination lock wouldn't open a big metal drop box in the lobby of a large office building, he wheeled the box onto his truck and took it back to the FedEx station, where he could cut open the metal and remove the envelopes and packages. And when Gerry Holland realized that an approaching storm made it too hazardous for him to drive his FedEx truck to the home of a customer who lived on a narrow bluff in the Great Smoky Mountains of Tennessee, he parked the vehicle and walked two miles to make the delivery on time.

In 1998 *Consumer Reports* found that FedEx achieved 97 percent reliability for making overnight deliveries during the peak season, when the challenge is the most daunting. FedEx's 97 percent contrasted with a stunningly low 65 percent for the United States Postal Service, which exemplified the common corporate culture of employees accepting that most obstacles couldn't be overcome and would absolve them from personal responsibility. No wonder FedEx had a 50 percent market share whereas the Postal Service had only 6 percent!

For Ray Kroc it was cleanliness, for Fred Smith it was reliability, and for an entrepreneur named Charles Schwab, the first virtue for running his company—and revolutionizing his industry—was ethics. Working in the stock brokerage business in the 1960s, "Chuck" was disillusioned by the pervasive corruption and conflict of interest. Stockbrokers were paid sales commissions rather than salaries, so they had an overwhelming incentive to get customers to trade stocks. Many brokers were utterly unscrupulous and would willingly sell bad stocks to their clients or pressure people to churn their portfolios even though it was wiser to hold on to good stocks for the longer run. What's more, the managers of the brokerage firms pressured their sales forces to recommend the stocks of companies that were the firm's biggest customers—companies that hired the firms to sell new issues of stocks and bonds that financed their expansion. It was a very cynical business: the brokerage firms operated under the guise of offering supposedly objective advice from well-meaning professionals that served the best interests of their small-time individual investors, but the reality was that these firms pushed biased advice that often served only their own interests and the interests of their big-time corporate customers.

So Chuck Schwab founded his own firm with the mission of being the most ethical brokerage in the world. He followed the Rule of One or Two, and ethical behavior was his first virtue. To walk the walk, he vowed that his people would all work on salary rather than commission, and they would never offer advice or try to "sell" stocks to customers. Instead of calling customers and pushing products at them, they would wait for the phone to ring and then take orders about what to buy or sell on the customers' behalf. And the new firm would serve only the individual investors rather than the corporate giants that paid multi-million-dollar fees and expected payback. Those measures would remove the hidden conflicts of interests that had corrupted the industry.

Chuck Schwab practiced his first virtue even though it meant passing up plenty of business—many customers wanted and expected advice—and it meant firing many employees who couldn't overcome the entrenched mind-set of the brokerage field. As John Kador quotes one of the company's managers in *Charles Schwab*: "Chuck ran a pretty loose outfit except for one thing. He didn't tolerate any funny business or unethical behavior. Integrity was critical. If you violated one of the compliance rules or did something illegal, you were out of there, no questions asked, even if we were super busy and needed every person we could get." The company tape-recorded all of its employees' telephone conversations with customers, and Chuck fired many brokers for giving advice or trying to "sell." The greatest test of how Chuck walked the walk came when he asked his eldest son, Charles Schwab Jr., whom he was grooming for a leadership role, to do a stint in the customer call center so he could understand the business firsthand. Charles Jr., known as "Sandy," couldn't refrain from offering stock-picking advice to customers, and so Chuck fired him from the position.

At many companies the "talk" and the "walk" are completely disconnected, and for a compelling reason: the people at these places are too embarrassed to name their first virtues. They need to say something that sounds benign because they can't say what's really happening. Take, for example, the rental-car business. The first virtue for those companies—Hertz, Avis, National, Dollar, Enterprise, and the rest—is selling insurance coverage to customers. That's the real source of their profits, not renting cars. At best they break even on the rentals. That extra daily charge for insurance is what brings in the actual profits. The big catch is that most customers don't really need to buy insurance, which is often provided free by their credit-card companies when they pay for the rental with their cards. So the trick to running a profitable rental-car business is to get your loyal customer-service agents to deceive and pressure people into buying something that's costly and unnecessary. The Rule of One or Two in car rentals is *sell insurance*.

But they can't say that—not openly, at least. It's so shameful that they can't even say it to their own employees—at least not in simple, clear words. But the employees need to get the message, and they do get it, very clearly, from how the company's managers walk the walk. In his book *Punching In*, Alex Frankel describes what it was like when he went through the official five-day training program for a job at Enterprise Rent-A-Car: "A good deal of our time in class was spent learning the nuances of signing customers up for this [insurance] coverage, and our training included learning how to counter customers' many objections." Although the trainer "told us that the company prides itself on being 'not in the rental-car business but in the customer-service business,' the customer-service section of the training binder was just ten pages, while the section on selling insurance was seventy-three pages—the longest section of the book. Though nobody at Enterprise said as much, it was quite clear that we were chiefly insurance salespeople." Even after his first week at Enterprise, Frankel wasn't taken in by the talk. He, like every other employee, looked at the walk as his crucial cue about what really mattered most.

Another company where the executives felt embarrassed to proclaim their real first virtue was Starbucks. Its founder, Howard Schulz, loved to talk the talk about how his patronage of espresso bars in Italy inspired "the Starbucks experience" of drinking the highest quality of freshly roasted coffee in the congenial atmosphere of a neighborhood café, were the regulars had a lively rapport with knowledgeable staffers who shared their passion for coffee. There's no doubt that Schulz really did want to change the way that Americans lived by teaching them to enjoy a more European concept of café culture. Schulz sincerely embraced those values. But they weren't his first virtues for Starbucks. His first virtues were rapid expansion and market dominance. Taylor Clark writes in his book *Starbucked* about a high-level meeting at headquarters in 1994, when "the question under discussion was straightforward: 'How can we become invulnerable?' Executives tossed in a variety of ideas for establishing the company as the planet's dominant coffee purveyor, but the conversation soon focused on one divisive proposal—that Starbucks should set a goal of opening two thousand stores by the year 2000. To many in the room, the idea seemed preposterous. At the time, Starbucks had only four hundred stores, so it would have to *quintuple* in size in just five years." But Schulz had a great belief in expansion, and he made it happen: "Starbucks didn't just hit two thousand by 2000; by the end of that year, it had almost *double* that, a total of thirty-five hundred coffee-houses." By 2007 the total had risen to more than thirteen thousand stores, and Starbucks controlled 73 percent of the specialty-coffeehouse market.

But then, in 2007, Howard Schulz wrote a memo to his executives that was leaked to the media. It was a remarkable document because it acknowledged that he, as a leader, had been forced to sacrifice many of Starbucks's key values for the sake of what he had enshrined as its *highest* value. He wrote: "Over the past ten years, in order to achieve the growth, development, and scale necessary to go from less than one thousand stores to thirteen thousand stores and beyond, we have had to make a series of decisions that, in retrospect, have led to the watering down of the Starbucks experience." In the beginning, he wrote, there was "romance and theater" when customers could look over the counter and watch the baristas making their drinks by hand on the old-fashioned La Marzocco espresso machines. The customers could chat with the baristas and cultivate friendships with them. However, for the sake of growth, Starbucks had needed to speed up the process, so Schulz had approved newer, taller machines that blocked the sightlines between the customers and the baristas, eliminating the possibility of Schulz's cherished "romance and theater."

In the beginning, Schulz wrote, the Starbucks employees scooped coffee beans out of bins and ground them fresh in front of the customers, which added to the sense of theater and filled the air with marvelous aromas. This practice was ended, too, in Starbucks's quest for growth, and so that heady coffee smell no longer pervaded the place. (In place of bins, Starbucks switched to "flavor-sealed" bags, which made it much easier to store the roasted beans and to ship them to a multitude of distant locations.)

In the beginning, Schulz wrote, Starbucks locations had "the warm feeling of a neighborhood store," but during the mania for expansion, which demanded lower costs and higher efficiencies, he had approved standardized designs that felt more like chain stores. "Some people even call our stores sterile, cookie cutter, no longer reflecting a passion our partners feel about our coffee," he wrote. "In fact, I am not sure people today even know we are roasting coffee. You certainly can't get that message being in our stores."

To his credit, Schultz added, "I take full responsibility myself" for these developments. But what's most revealing about the memo is that Schulz himself seems genuinely surprised to discover that the way he walked the walk for two decades didn't reflect the way that he talked the talk. He did what real leaders have to do: follow the Rule of One or Two. But his real first virtue didn't sound as noble as the values it trumped. Schulz couldn't tell reporters, "We're sacrificing the customer experience for the sake of massive expansion." And he couldn't even acknowledge this truth to himself.

Leaders who strive to create cultural, social, and political change need to practice the Rule of One or Two as well. Eleanor Roosevelt understood it brilliantly. Her first virtue for herself—and for the rest of America's women—was independence. That meant that women needed to make their own money and have their own political voice and power. Eleanor herself decided to become financially independent in 1928 as she rebounded from her emotional devastation after learning of her husband's extramarital affair. In that era, political wives were expected to remain mutely in the background, but Eleanor soon achieved her own high profile—and high income—from voicing her own very specific and strong opinions as she wrote articles for magazines, delivered lectures, and appeared on radio shows. In 1933, when Franklin Roosevelt began his first term in the White House, Eleanor resolved that she would earn as much as his seventy-five-thousand-dollar salary for being president.

In the following five years she published six books and a slew of articles—and she often disagreed publicly with FDR's policies, beginning early in his first term. As a cost-cutting measure, FDR signed a law that would fire thousands of married women who were employed by the federal government. The reasoning was that their husbands already provided the family an income, even though the Department of Labor found that nine out of ten of these women needed their jobs in the hard times of the Great Depression—and many of their families wound up foreclosing on their mortgages or depleting their life savings to survive. Eleanor Roosevelt was outraged, and she called the policy "a very bad and very foolish thing" in the pages of the *New York Times*.

"It was astounding and unprecedented for a First Lady to protest her husband's legislation," writes her biographer Blanche Wiesen Cook. Even now, seven decades later, no other First Lady has dared to do so. Even the famously strong and opinionated

Hillary Rodham Clinton was careful to maintain a united front in her public statements during and after her husband's presidency. But Eleanor Roosevelt routinely criticized Franklin's decisions in her articles, books, and speeches—all of which she insisted on writing herself, without the aid of ghostwriters—as well as in her interviews and radio appearances. In 1938 she even published a best-selling book devoted entirely to her sharp criticisms of FDR's foreign policy. For his part, Franklin calmly accepted her frequent outbursts of public opposition, telling her on one occasion: "Lady, this is a free country. Say what you think. If you get me in Dutch, I'll get myself out. Anyway, the whole world knows I can't control you."

The whole world knew it, and most Americans loved it. In 1939 the Gallup Poll showed that Eleanor had an even higher approval rating with voters (67 percent) than Franklin did. In a poll in 1947, Eleanor was named "the woman most admired by other American women." Through her own personal example she showed them what was possible: she proved that a woman could be just as strong, opinionated, forceful, and ambitious as her husband—even if her husband was the president of the United States of America. "ER saw her own struggle for independence as connected to the wider struggle for full economic and political power for all women," writes her biographer, Cook.

One of the twentieth century's greatest leaders, Nelson Mandela, grasped the importance of practicing first virtues. When he became his nation's president in 1994, he knew that "the future peace of South Africa would depend on forgiveness," writes his biographer Anthony Sampson. For years the nation had been plagued with violence and threatened with civil war. Mandela needed to forge a peaceful reconciliation between the black majority, which had finally achieved power for the first time in the new democratic regime of "one person, one vote," and the Dutch-descended Afrikaner minority, which had brutally repressed them during its many decades of ruling. That seemed like a nearly impossible challenge. Mandela needed to make South Africans believe it was possible, and he did so through his own extraordinary personal example.

He was an unlikely peacemaker. Mandela had a history of youthful militancy. Imposing at six foot two, he had been an amateur heavyweight boxer in his early days, and he had headed (albeit briefly and incompetently) a guerrilla group that committed acts of sabotage. And he was a man with reason to hate: he had spent twenty-seven years and six months in prison serving a life sentence. But when he finally emerged at the age of seventy-one, he showed again and again that even he could forgive the brutal enemies who had imprisoned him, even though they included, in his own words, "all sorts of people whose hands are dripping with blood."

And still he forgave them: "Mandela went out of his way to conciliate his ex-enemies in a succession of symbolic visits with a high sense of drama," writes Sampson. "Mandela welcomed many old opponents from his jail years. When Niel Barnard retired as head of intelligence, Mandela gave a dinner party for him in Pretoria, with guests including General Willemse, the former commander of Robben Island," the prison colony where

Mandela spent seventeen years living in a seven-foot-by-eight-foot cell with only one tiny window, doing hard labor breaking rocks in a lime quarry and subsisting on corn gruel. Mandela appointed one of his former prison wardens to a prestigious ambassadorship. He hosted a lunch for the prosecutor who had made "vindictive and hectoring tirades" during his trial. And as John Carlin describes in his book *Playing the Enemy*, Mandela became a great fan and public supporter of South Africa's rugby team, the Springboks, which had been seen as a symbol of white oppression by the nation's black population. As the Springboks readied to play in the world championship game, Mandela stunned the crowd of ninety thousand in the stadium by coming onto the field wearing one of the team's green jerseys. Symbolically, his act was much like a freed American slave dressing in a Confederate soldier's uniform while saluting the Confederate flag during the playing of the "Battle Hymn of the Republic." The white audience, astonished by the gesture, erupted into a chant of "Nelson, Nelson!"

So far we've looked at some of the greatest of all societal and political leaders—Martin Luther King Jr., Eleanor Roosevelt, and Nelson Mandela—as well as some of the most successful business leaders of recent generations: Jeff Bezos of Amazon. com, Sidney Weinberg of Goldman Sachs, Herb Kelleher and Colleen Barrett of Southwest Airlines, Danny Meyer of the Union Square Cafe, Ray Kroc and Fred Turner of McDonald's, Fred Smith of FedEx, Chuck Schwab of Charles Schwab, and Howard Schulz of Starbucks. But the Rule of One or Two applies equally to leaders of companies, teams, and movements of all kinds and sizes. One of my favorite stories about the power of first virtues is about the head coach of the varsity football team at Westminster, the Christian high school in Atlanta that my wife, Susan, attended.

The autumn of 1992 was Gerry Romberg's first season coaching the Westminster Wildcats. The team lost the first six games—its worst start ever in the school's history. The Westminster community wasn't accustomed to losing. The previous year the Wildcats had started the season with a winning streak. Many of the school's alumni still talked about the team's golden era under the legendary coach Charlie Brake, who achieved an exceptional record of 129 wins, 54 losses, and 8 ties between 1956 and 1972. That's the kind of performance they expected from Romberg. Westminster was one of the wealthiest private schools in the nation, and its community felt entitled to be winners. People were already speculating that Romberg wouldn't last very long as head coach.

In October one of the varsity football players showed up at the homecoming dance noticeably drunk—an embarrassing situation that forced the school's officials to take action. It wasn't just that drinking under the age of twenty-one was illegal. The school's discipline policy banned students from drinking on campus or off, and the school's athletes had all signed contracts pledging that they wouldn't drink or smoke during the season. Westminster was a Christian school, and its administrators were serious about their mission. If you listed Westminster's first virtues at the time, they would have been:

No. 1: Christian ideals of character
No. 2: academic excellence

So it was obvious that the school would have to take some kind of disciplinary action against the drunken football player—probably kicking him off the squad for the rest of the season. Coach Romberg called an emergency meeting of the team. Before they assembled, though, many of the players conferred with each other and devised their own strategy for the confrontation. A group of twenty players, mostly juniors and seniors, decided that they would all confess together that they had consumed alcohol that season, too. Surely the coach couldn't field a team without twenty of his most experienced and valuable players. By acting in solidarity, the players expected that they would be the ones to hold power in this situation, not Coach Romberg. Surely the first-year coach couldn't risk losing the rest of the games in the season, which might mean that he would lose his job.

Gerry Romberg convened the emergency meeting, and he asked the team: Who among you has had an alcoholic drink this season? The cabal of twenty players all raised their hands. Without hesitation, Romberg kicked them all off the team for the season. He upheld the Rule of One or Two, and winning at football was neither No. 1 nor No. 2.

That Saturday only thirty-nine out of Westminster's fifty-nine players were allowed to put on their uniforms for the game against rival Eagle's Landing. Ten of Westminster's players were making their first varsity starts. One of these ten novices was Hunter Hill, a freshman, who had to initiate the action on the field as quarterback, the most important offensive position. Hill was nervous as the game began, but he performed extremely well: he ran for three touchdowns and passed for a fourth. Westminster won by a score of 42 to 14.

"It feels like we just won the state championship," Coach Romberg told a reporter for the *Atlanta Journal-Constitution*, which carried the embarrassing news of the twenty suspensions. "Under the circumstances, it makes our first win much sweeter."

The following year, my wife, Susan, was a senior at Westminster, and she often went to parties at classmates' homes, where just about everyone was drinking—except for the football players. The coach's leadership had changed the way that his players acted. And eventually they became winners once again: after posting losing records for his first two seasons, Coach Romberg guided the team to eight consecutive years of making the playoffs. In 1996 they reached the Georgia State semifinals at the Georgia Dome. They had five blockbuster seasons with ten or more wins, and in 2004 they achieved the first undefeated regular season in the school's history. In 2005 Romberg enjoyed his one-hundredth career win at Westminster, and by 2008 he was within close range of eclipsing his legendary predecessor and becoming the winningest varsity football coach in the school's history.

Chapter Four

When You Walk the Walk,
You Share the Struggle and the Risk

In 1970 Bill Hewlett faced a difficult economic situation that would test the strength of his conviction in the values that he and his cofounder, Dave Packard, had instilled in the culture of their company. It had come about unexpectedly: only the previous year, the outlook for American business had seemed so promising. The 1960s had been booming years. To the corporate chiefs of that time, it had seemed certain "the greatest advance of prosperity the nation had ever known" (as it was called by *Time* magazine) would sustain its momentum. Dave Packard felt so comfortable about the state of the business that he accepted an offer to move from Palo Alto, California, to Washington, D.C., to serve in the government, leaving Hewlett-Packard's sixteen thousand employees to Bill Hewlett's sole stewardship.

But then, in early 1970, America lurched from prosperity to recession. The governors of the Federal Reserve, worried that inflation was on the verge of racing out of control, slammed the brakes on the speeding economy: they tightened credit for banks, pushing interest rates to the highest level in more than a hundred years. Companies couldn't afford to borrow the cash they needed, and so they shuttered factories: one-quarter of America's industrial capacity lay idle. They pared their outlays for advertising and for promising research and development projects. The biggest industries had an awful year. The airlines struggled because many companies cut back on business travel and families postponed taking expensive vacations. Detroit cut its annual production of cars from 8.2 million to 6.5 million. The nation's largest railroad, Penn Central, went bankrupt in the biggest corporate collapse in history. America's corporate profits tumbled to the lowest rate in a decade. The Dow Jones stock market index fell to an eight-year low. Unemployment shot up from 3.9 percent to 5.8 percent. When *Time*'s editors looked back at the end of 1970, they wrote: "It was the year of the layoff."

And it was the year of the layoff even for the technological whiz kids of Silicon Valley. Even though America was still immersed in the Vietnam War, the Pentagon began deep cuts in its spending, which shocked many northern California electronics companies that relied on defense contracts, including Hewlett-Packard. Everyone needed to cut their operating costs to get their companies through the downturn. Many of the chief executive officers presided over layoffs of thousands of their rank-and-file workers as their way of reducing expenses. Meanwhile these CEOs and their top executives held tightly to their own positions and privileges, their high pay and enviable perks.

That wasn't Bill Hewlett's idea of how real leaders were supposed to act. He knew that leaders had to share the struggle with their people. And that's what he decided to do. Hewlett asked for every HP employee to take one unpaid day off every two weeks. And that meant everyone, from himself and his top executives to the receptionists and the janitors. They would all accept a 10 percent reduction in their pay until the company's fortunes rebounded. The whole place would simply shut down every other Friday. Bill Hewlett explained the idea in a memo to all HP employees: "Usually in business, it is the little guy on the line who takes it on the chin, while management and higher-ups stay at work," he wrote. "It is only right that everyone share in the pain, up and down the line."

The "nine-day fortnight," as it became known, was an extraordinary success. "Looking back, it was Bill Hewlett's most brilliant invention as a business executive," writes Michael S. Malone in *Bill & Dave*, his history of the company. "Inside HP, where many employees had already resigned themselves to an inevitable layoff, the Nine-Day Fortnight plan produced an upwelling of gratitude, even love, for Hewlett-Packard—and Bill Hewlett in particular—that would carry the company through the next two decades, and would attach to Bill Hewlett for the rest of his life." Rather than laying off one-tenth of the company's workforce—which would have meant cutting sixteen hundred workers at a time when it would have been very hard for them to find other good jobs—Bill Hewlett's leadership had strengthened their loyalty. When America's economy began rebounding, HP's reputation was invaluable: the company was in a position to hire the best people as it built up its workforce from sixteen thousand in 1970 to sixty-seven thousand in 1981.

Hewlett's decisive move illustrates the concept of first virtues that I discussed in the last two chapters. After three decades of "talking the talk" about how HP prized all of its employees—their skills, knowledge, experience, and creativity—as its greatest asset, Hewlett kept "walking the walk" by doing whatever it took to hold on to every worker rather than resorting to harsh layoffs. And his decision is also a classic example of what I'm going to discuss in this chapter: leaders must share the struggle. That's a simple and powerful principle that seems to have been foolishly ignored by so many of the ambitious individuals who have aspired to leadership roles in our time. Sharing the struggle, the risk, and the hardship is one of the most crucial things you do when you walk the walk.

Al Gore did everything possible to be a leader—except sharing the struggle.

He flew around the country hundreds of times to rally audiences to take action now and confront the crisis of global warming. He reached millions of people through his Oscar-winning documentary and best-selling book, *An Inconvenient Truth*. He conveyed a sense of great urgency. He spoke with intelligence and conviction. He trained more than one thousand people, from the actress Cameron Diaz in Hollywood to the clerks at Wal-Mart in midwestern towns, to give his PowerPoint presentation to their friends and neighbors. He helped mount "Live Earth" rock concerts around the world to focus attention on the crisis. And yet, in his own life, he still lived as though global warming weren't really a problem, let alone an urgent one.

Al Gore and his wife, Tipper, resided in a 10,000-square-foot neoclassical mansion, a white-pillared *Gone with the Wind* fantasy in Nashville's exclusive Belle Mead district. It was four times the size of the average American house, and it consumed twelve times as much energy as the typical house in the city of Nashville. The Gores' energy bills averaged twelve hundred dollars a month.

If Al Gore were a real leader, he would have sold the palatial Belle Mead house and moved into a cute little bungalow. He would downsize to the average square footage of the American house circa 1970 (1,500 square feet) or, better yet, circa 1950 (983 square feet). He'd pick a cozy cottage in an urban neighborhood, where he could leave the car in the driveway and do all his errands on foot. Then he could invite some of his billionaire friends to visit, such as Apple's Steve Jobs and Google's Sergey Brin and Larry Page, and show them his new lifestyle and suggest that they live that way, too. And he could write articles for *Vanity Fair* and *People* explaining why the smaller house hasn't been a sacrifice—in fact, it has liberated him and made him much happier now. And he could challenge the *New York Times*'s Thomas L. Friedman, the most influential columnist of our era and one of the loudest voices of concern about global warming, to give up his own 11,400-square-foot house and move into a cozy little bungalow, too.

But that's not what Gore was doing as his book and movie put him in the spotlight in early 2007. Gore was supposed to be the star witness at the United States Senate's hearings about climate change, but his testimony was upstaged when a Republican senator mentioned the wastefulness of his huge home. Soon after, Gore did what he could to make the monster somewhat more energy efficient: he put solar panels on the roof, installed new windows, and switched to compact fluorescent lightbulbs. But any architect could have told him that a 10,000-square-foot house tricked out with every ecological feature would still consume more energy than the most conventional 5,000-square-foot McMansion, let alone a 1,000-square-foot bungalow.

If Al Gore, the self-styled Mr. Environment himself, wouldn't scale back to a smaller house, then why should the rest of us? With that kind of "leadership," it's no wonder that Americans weren't making the dramatic changes in their lifestyles that would actually prevent catastrophe.

With that kind of "leadership," it's no wonder that Ted Turner's daughter, Laura Turner Seydel, was able to convince major newspapers and magazines to run splashy articles hyping her supposed "EcoManor" in Atlanta, a hulking 6,200-square-footer. "'EcoManor' Makes an Earth-friendly Statement," crowed the *Atlanta Journal-Constitution*. "The First Certifiably Green Mansion" proclaimed *Fortune*, which noted that the house had met the guidelines set forth by the U.S. Green Building Council. The articles fawned over the solar roof panels, "energy-efficient appliances," and "soy-based insulation" in the five-bedroom, seven-bathroom structure. The reality is that the EcoManor was two to three times as large as the other houses on its block—and would use more energy than any of them. What's worse, its hulking size ruined the modest scale of the street, where for decades some of Atlanta's most affluent residents—doctors, lawyers, executives—had been happy to raise their families amid understated good taste. My wife, Susan, grew up in that neighborhood, and her closest childhood friend lived across the street from the lot that eventually gave rise to the EcoManor. At a party, I talked with most of the neighbors on the block, and they were united in their hatred for the Seydel's oversized edifice, which they called the "EgoManor." They told me that its excessive bulk cast shadows that made it impossible for the next-door neighbor to grow her garden.

The ugliest irony was that the Seydels kept an equally large house nearby while at first they told neighbors that the EcoManor would be their guesthouse: a 6,200-square-foot, five-bedroom, seven-bathroom "guesthouse." The reality was that they built it as a prototype of the Eco McMansions they hoped to develop throughout the nation. And why wouldn't wealthy Americans delude themselves into thinking that they were taking part in a noble cause when they were actually worsening the situation? Al Gore was their "leader." They shared Al Gore's sacrifice, which wasn't much of a sacrifice.

Mark Fields was supposed to be the long-awaited leader who would save the American auto industry—but he wouldn't walk the walk by sharing the struggle with his people.

The Ford Motor Company was losing billions of dollars a year. It desperately needed to change. And so, in 2005, Ford appointed Mark Fields as president of its North American operation, which was the most troubled part of the global company. Fields quickly created a turnaround plan called the "Way Forward." It meant eliminating forty-four thousand jobs—more than one-fifth the workforce—and closing fourteen manufacturing plants. And Fields proposed cutting health-care benefits for the blue-collar workers who remained. He stressed the sense of urgency with his new slogan, "Change or Die," which he posted on the gates to the factories. As part of his case for change, he told Ford Motor's employees that they would have to share in the sacrifices to save the company.

But Mark Fields himself didn't share in the sacrifices. For cutting costs so fiercely, Ford Motor's chief executive Bill Ford rewarded Fields with a $2.3 million bonus. That lifted Fields's yearly pay to $5.6 million. Rather than moving to Detroit and living among his colleagues as a full-fledged member of their community, Fields kept his family in Delray Beach, Florida, and commuted every weekend on the company's private jet. The flights cost Ford Motor $215,000 for the last three months of 2005. When a local television station ran an exposé, Ford's employees were outraged: "I don't think that anyone south of MF on the org chart is listening. If you were a fly on the wall inside the offices of these megalomaniacs you'd see that it's not only 'business as usual,' it's gotten worse," wrote one employee.

Is there any wonder why no one listened to Mark Fields—or followed him?

There was a time when being a leader meant going first. Leaders shared the struggle with their followers. They fought with us on the front lines.

I mean that literally. John Keegan, the foremost historian of warfare, writes that for "a hundred generations," from ancient times through the nineteenth century, the greatest military commanders fought side by side with their soldiers, subjecting themselves to the same terrifying risks that they asked of their troops. "The first and greatest imperative of command is to be present in person," Keegan explains in *The Mask of Command.* "Those who impose risk must be seen to share it."

I believe that this first virtue for leaders in the military is equally vital for leaders in business, politics, social activism, or any other civilian realm. Before we look at more examples of corporate leaders who, like Bill Hewlett, have walked the walk by sharing the struggle and risk with their people, let's take a whirlwind tour through twenty-five hundred years of military history for some dramatic illustrations of this idea.

"The first and greatest imperative of command" was well understood by Alexander the Great, who always took his place front and center among his troops in combat. His body was covered with wounds inflicted by every weaponry technology of his time: swords, lances, darts, arrows, stones, and catapulted missiles. He was seriously injured several times, and once he was nearly killed in battle. And his conspicuous example inspired his men: "The knowledge that their king was taking the supreme risk drove capable and well-briefed subordinates, at the head of drilled and self-confident troops, to fight as hard and skillfully as if he had been at the elbow of each of them," Keegan writes.

Alexander's practice of walking the walk helped put down a nascent mutiny. In a famous incident in 324 BCE at Opis, near present-day Baghdad, when Alexander's efforts to include large numbers of Persian troops into his armies were sparking a revolt among his soldiers from his Greek homeland, he silenced the angry crowd with this speech, an accurate account of how he had shared their "exertions and hardships": "Is any of you aware of having endured more for me than I for him?" Alexander asked. "Come now, any of you with wounds—let him strip off and show them, and I shall show mine in turn. In my case, there is no part of my body—not the front, in any case—that has been left without a wound, and there is no kind of weapon, be it for hand-to-hand fighting or throwing, whose scars I do not have on myself. I have sword gashes from hand-to-hand fighting, arrow wounds, injuries from artillery projectiles, and I have been struck in many places by stones and clubs. All this for you and your glory and your riches, as I take you triumphant through every land and sea, over the rivers, mountains and plains."

The troops knew from their own experience at his side in many battles that their king and commander was speaking truthfully. If anything, Alexander (as told in this account from the Roman historian Arrian) had stoically downplayed the fierce drama of his history of battle scars. When he mentioned being "struck in many places by stones" and receiving "sword gashes," he left out that the blows had come to his head, which was "split open by a barbarian dagger" (in the words of the Roman historian Plutarch). Alexander casually refers to "arrow wounds" and "projectiles," but he doesn't give a complete report about how one especially large arrow, shot from an enemy's catapult, was so forceful that it went through both his shield and his breastplate and impaled his chest "deep enough to cover the metal head," as Plutarch wrote. And Alexander spared the gruesome details about when his thigh was slit and his shinbone split open. Still, his oration had a powerful effect on his troops, who fell silent—and ended their rebellion.

As the dominance of Greece gave way to the ascendance of Rome, these lessons of leadership were well remembered. Julius Caesar marched together with his men, ate the same food they ate, and generally shared their hardships for the seven years they spent in their conquest of Gaul (the vast expanse of today's France, Holland, Belgium, and parts of western Germany). And when Caesar was confronted by crisis, he would put his own life at conspicuous risk. That's what happened in 57 BCE, when Caesar's forces were losing a battle against the Belgian tribes of the Nervians. In his *Commentaries on the Gallic War*, Caesar wrote that many of his army's centurions (officers who led groups of eighty men) had been killed or wounded. "The rest of the men were slowing down, and some in the rear ranks had given up fighting and were intent on getting out of range of the enemy," which kept pursuing them relentlessly. In response, Caesar "recognized that this was a crisis," and he upheld the first and greatest imperative of command: "I had no shield with me but I snatched one from a soldier in the rear ranks and went forward to the front line," he wrote. "Once there, I called out to all the centurions by name and shouted encouragement to the rest of the men." The result: "My arrival gave the troops fresh hope.

Their determination was restored. . . ." Caesar's army wound up winning the battle and completing its conquest of what's now Belgium and northeastern France.

After the fall of Rome, a millennium of medieval warfare was premised on this first virtue of leaders sharing the struggle and risk. The English army of Henry V defeated a French force several times its size at Agincourt in 1415 with the youthful king risking his own life throughout the legendary battle. That's why Shakespeare had total credibility when he wrote one of his most famous lines: the Henry character saying "we band of brothers." Henry truly acted as though he were their brother, not their overlord.

When history's long reign of monarchy eventually yielded to the tentative rise of democracy, the new egalitarian spirit made it especially important for military leaders to be seen sharing the struggle and risk with their citizen-soldiers. The biographer Joseph J. Ellis writes that George Washington, as commander in chief of America's Revolutionary army, "personally led the assault across the [Delaware] river in a driving sleet storm and was in the vanguard of the attack on the garrison of Hessian mercenaries at Trenton." While Washington didn't always risk his own life at the front lines, like Caesar he grasped when especially difficult situations required the leader's personal example.

Like Alexander and his Greek troops two millennia earlier, Washington's many years of sharing the struggle and risk gave him a powerful emotional bond with his men that helped him curtail an incipient revolt when the soldiers were rightfully angered by their predicament. In *For Liberty and Glory*, the historian James R. Gaines recounts a pivotal moment in 1783 when the new nation's officer corps "very nearly dissolved in mutiny" because the government owed them around $5 million in back pay. Washington supported the officers' claims, but he needed to prevent a revolt. He delivered a speech to them to explain why Congress was being inexcusably slow to take action. When he saw that his prepared remarks weren't calming the angry, agitated crowd, he reached into his pocket and took out a letter from a congressman that explained the legislative morass. In order to read them the letter, Washington also took out a pair of eyeglasses. "This was new to Washington's officers, who had never seen him in spectacles," Gaines writes. "Hearing a rustle in the audience as he put them on, he thought to say, 'Gentlemen, you must pardon me. I have grown gray in the service of my country and now find myself growing blind.'"

This unplanned sentence had a profound impact: it "movingly reminded his audience that every day of the past eight years had required of their commander in chief great personal sacrifice, relentless dedication to the cause, and unremitting hard work," Gaines writes. When Washington left the room, "some officers were discreetly drying their eyes." And then the assembly of officers "unanimously passed a resolution declaring their gratitude toward him and their commitment to continued negotiations with Congress. Once again, Washington had held the Continental Army together."

In the nineteenth century, the most momentous military victory—Napoléon Bonaparte's final defeat, at Waterloo, by Britain's Duke of Wellington—was a classic example of the influence of a leader who shared the struggle and risk. While Napoléon watched from atop a hill at the edge of the valley, the Duke of Wellington rode horseback through the front lines, hazarding musket fire over the course of many hours, willingly subjecting himself to even greater danger than that faced by many of his officers and their men.

"Wellington's energy was legendary; so too was his attention to detail, unwillingness to delegate, ability to do without sleep or food, disregard for personal comfort, contempt for danger," writes John Keegan. "But in the four days of the Waterloo campaign he surpassed even his own stringent standards of courage and asceticism. He slept, for example, hardly at all." Wellington "was constantly in the soldiers' range of vision," and even though the battle line was two miles long, nearly all of his men saw him in action. "That Wellington had borne a greater share of danger than his subordinates is unarguable," Keegan writes. "Whenever the pressure of attack had flowed from one section of the line to another, he had followed it, leaving the units he had supervised to a respite of which he had none at all." That's how Wellington delivered the final defeat to the emperor who had conquered and ruled the European continent.

The tradition of military leadership that spanned twenty-four centuries from Alexander to Wellington, a tradition of commanders who shared the struggle, was interrupted in World War I. On the western front, the generals lived in utter safety and luxury at some of Europe's grandest castles, far away from the horrific trenches where their soldiers suffered, fought, and died. They became known derisively as the "château generals."

Lord Moran, a British doctor who fought in the war, writes in *The Anatomy of Courage* that he and his fellow soldiers never actually saw the generals who had sent them to the front.

The result was that large portions of every army ultimately revolted or simply deserted. In May 1917 nearly half the divisions of the French army put down their arms, Keegan writes, "announcing their unwillingness to attack the Germans again until their grievances were addressed. In October of that year the Russian army, disillusioned by the pointlessness of its suffering, simply 'voted for peace with its feet,' as Lenin put it, allowing him to transform the power vacuum which resulted into political revolution."

The crisis of leadership continued in the aftermath of the war. In 1932 the so-called Bonus Expeditionary Force of twenty thousand World War I veterans and their families camped in a shantytown across a bridge from Washington, D.C., in an effort to convince President Herbert Hoover to give them the bonuses that the government had promised them many years earlier but had not yet paid. They were deserving, and they were needy: it was during the Great Depression, and many of them were homeless and impoverished. But in an ignominious move, Hoover ordered the army to repel these veterans. He sent cavalrymen wielding sabers and infantrymen brandishing rifles, all backed up by tanks. Hoover's troops teargassed and bayoneted the unarmed veterans, who didn't fight back.

Eleanor Roosevelt felt horrified by what she called a "tragedy." Later that year, after her husband, Franklin Delano Roosevelt, succeeded Hoover as president, the World War I veterans set up camp once again to demand their bonus—and, this time, to protest how FDR was cutting their benefits. Although FDR dispatched an aide, supposedly to negotiate with the veterans, he had no intention of paying them, and they weren't fooled whatsoever by the move. "They didn't believe there was a dime's worth of difference between Hoover and Roosevelt," writes the historian Blanche Weisen Cook.

That was before Eleanor Roosevelt asserted her own leadership. Acting independently, against the wishes of Franklin's advisers, Eleanor visited the veterans' campsite, where she had to "wade through ankle-deep mud to visit the marchers' living quarters," Cook writes. The veterans gathered in a big tent, where "she addressed the group and apologized for the fact that she could tell them nothing about the bonus. But she had seen the war, toured the battlefields, and understood their anger." Even though, as a woman, she couldn't have fought with them at the front, she had contributed behind the lines: she "had driven a truck through the railway yards in the cold of night, and talked with the boys as they left. She had served coffee and prepared sandwiches for these young men, eager to go into the unknown. And she had seen them when they returned, hobbling on crutches or carried off the trains, and had visited them in hospitals."

The veterans interrupted Eleanor Roosevelt's speech with cheers, and afterward they "waved her off with songs." Even though Franklin still wouldn't pay their promised bonus, in Eleanor they had found someone who had shared their struggle, seen it firsthand, understood them, and promised to continue struggling for them. Like Alexander the Great and George Washington before her, Eleanor Roosevelt could quell a revolt because her past actions proved her sincere commitment to the people. "ER had helped to renew their faith," Cook writes. "The First Lady would fight for their interests."

The Second World War marked a rediscovery of the first imperative of leadership. Lord Moran, who had become Winston Churchill's personal physician, writes in *Churchill at War 1940– 1945* about traveling with the British leader near the North African front. Prime Minister Churchill, Lord Moran, and General Sir Harold Alexander all camped out in tents "like those of gypsies on a heath," Moran writes. "Commanders-in-Chief no longer live in comfort, as they did in chateaux in France in the First World War. It is not that they fear attacks from the air, but rather that they dread democracy. They want to persuade the soldiery that their leaders are not lounging in luxury while they grovel in discomfort."

Some of America's most decisive turnarounds in World War II were inspired by leaders who shared the struggle and risk. In the Pacific theater, for example, General Douglas MacArthur received reports of the terrible morale of America's 32nd Infantry Division in the jungles of New Guinea in November 1942. The soldiers refused to fight anymore, leaving the battle stalemated. MacArthur sent a new commander there, Lieutenant General Robert L. Eichelberger, who found the men "tired, riddled with malaria, and demoralized," writes the West Point military historian Cole C. Kingseed in *Old Glory Stories: American Combat Leadership in World War II*. The troops were half-starved, sick,

and ragged. Before Eichelberger himself toured the front lines
on foot, their "leaders" had never been there or seen firsthand
the awful conditions. Eichelberger quickly replaced these commanders, and he gave the troops their first hot meals in weeks.
He established his command post within 125 yards of the front
line—hardly more than the length of a football field away from
the deadly fire. And then he resumed the battle.

The troops, who had refused to fight, now rallied under
Eichelberger's leadership. "The effect of his presence was electric," Kingseed writes. Within a month they won "the first significant land victory against the Japanese" despite suffering
terrible casualties. Eichelberger himself cheated death when he
was shot at, and missed, by an enemy soldier only fifteen yards
away. Still, the new commander, who was fifty-six years old, lost
thirty pounds in a month from living and fighting in the ma-
larial jungle. He had shared the struggle.

A similar turnaround took place in the European theater under Major General Lucian K. Truscott Jr., who was assigned to
take command on the Italian front at the Anzio beachhead in
January 1944. The American troops were under air and artillery
attack by the Germans, and their morale was low. Truscott found
that the men in the lower ranks felt that their commanders "were
unduly concerned for their own safety." The commanders stayed
in headquarters far from the front lines in deep caverns or underground shelters, where they studied maps rather than seeing
the battles firsthand.

Truscott visited his troops on the front lines every day. "The
appearance of the commanding general quickly galvanized the

beleaguered defenders of the beachhead," Kingseed writes. His conspicuous presence quickly restored the unit's confidence and optimism. Under his leadership they stopped the Germans' advance and held the beach.

Why did it make such a powerful difference to the men whether their commander led from the front or stayed in the safety of the back? It showed the officer's "unwillingness to order them to do that which he would not do," writes Gerald F. Linderman in *The World Within War,* his fascinating study of soldiers' psychology in World War II. "Here was the assurance both that he would not needlessly risk the lives of others and that he regarded the existence of the men as no less valuable than his own. This tacit recognition of soldiers as equivalent persons was the key requisite of leadership in the field."

How did the most effective officers in World War II make their men feel like their equals? Linderman writes that they "minimized all resort to rank" and "seemed most willing to renounce their authority." Instead of relying on the supposed power of their position, they led by the real power of their example. The ordinary soldiers had a natural suspicion of the officers, who could earn their trust only by showing real concern for their welfare and by sharing the same hard conditions and risks. Officers had to lead by walking the walk, and that was impossible to fake: "Soldiers never failed to detect and despise the false 'we,'" Linderman writes. But when there was a true "we," when the leaders and their men considered themselves a real "band of brothers," the results could be extraordinary.

America's best military leaders since World War II have all understood these lessons. Consider the experience of Norman Schwarzkopf, who gained renown in 1991 as the top field commander of the Gulf War. Schwarzkopf learned the first imperative of command in his first assignment after graduating from West Point in 1957. He began his legendary military career as a second lieutenant in the 101st Airborne Division at Fort Campbell, Kentucky. In his memoir, he writes that the division had a "magnificent tradition": its paratroopers had jumped behind German lines on D-day in World War II, and they included the men whose heroic exploits were retold in *Band of Brothers*, the best-selling book and HBO television miniseries. But there in Kentucky, more than a decade later, the young Schwarzkopf found himself reporting to a captain who was "afraid to jump." The captain would get them up at four in the morning for practice jumps but he was always coming up with excuses for why he wouldn't take part, such as claiming to have the flu. Then the captain would drive to the drop zone, so if necessary he could pretend that he had parachuted along with the rest of them: "If someone from battle group headquarters came by to inspect, he would make a show of brushing dirt off himself. The inspectors bought it; the troops didn't; they knew he was afraid. If those men had had amoebic dysentery they wouldn't have followed him to the latrine."

Schwarzkopf learned from that mockery of leadership, but he also had positive role models on his way to becoming a general. In 1976 Schwarzkopf was assigned to lead the first infantry brigade at Fort Lewis, "the one nobody wanted," he writes. It was called "the circus brigade." Its performance was "a disgrace." And Schwarzkopf himself was soon assigned a new superior, Major General Richard Cavazos, a Korean War hero, who "had a reputation as an inspiring leader and trainer," Schwarzkopf writes. "Cavazos got our attention right away: on the morning of his first commander's conference, I pulled up to division headquarters in my jeep and noticed a commotion in the parking lot. The general had intercepted the commander of the Army hospital, had ordered him to raise the jeep's hood, and was under there checking the engine for grime. I beat it into the building as fast as I could, before he decided to inspect *my* jeep. Overnight, the equipment maintenance in the 9th Division took a quantum leap."

The circus brigade wound up leading its division in maintenance statistics and every other measure of performance. General Cavazos could have taken a more conventional approach. The general could have given a speech about the importance of maintenance, or simply issued an order, which would have been passed down to some lowly inspector, who would issue reports that no one would pay attention to or enforce. But by doing it himself, he showed that he really cared, it was really important to him.

Schwarzkopf found another exemplar of leadership in Brigadier General Willard Latham. Like Cavazos, he had also fought in the Korean War, where he saw men being captured or killed by the Chinese because they weren't fit enough and couldn't keep up with a fast retreat across a river. Years later, as a commander in the Vietnam War, Latham decided that all his people—including Schwarzkopf—should be able to run five miles in fifty minutes.

"That shook up headquarters something terrible, because most of those colonels hadn't exercised in years," Schwarzkopf writes. "But within days they were out there, huffing and puffing and getting into shape. There was no way for them to fake it, either: Latham worked out right alongside them. . . . I sensed this was a man I could learn from."

Schwarzkopf appreciated all these lessons on the first imperative of command. He had also learned from experience as he succeeded at a series of difficult assignments in his rise through the ranks. In 1968, when Schwarzkopf took over command of the First Battalion of the Sixth Infantry in the Vietnam War, the outgoing commander gave him a bottle of Johnny Walker Black scotch and said, "You're gonna need it," assuring him that it was a "lousy battalion" with "lousy morale" and a "lousy mission." Schwarzkopf soon discovered that it was indeed a failing outfit that was losing lives, and why "the First of the Sixth" was justly called "the Worst of the Sixth." He soon came to think it might be the worst battalion in the United States Army. In his memoir he recalls his first day: "By the time I got to the mess hall there was a long line—troops standing in the rain, [officers] bossing them around. I took my place at the end of the line, which caused a mess sergeant to trot over. 'Sir, you don't have to stand in line. We've got a special section for officers.'

"'Sergeant,' I said, 'if my troops have to stand in line out here in the rain, I'll stand here, too.' He seemed confused by that and went away. Meanwhile the troops were staring at me." One soldier told him: "'This is the first time we've ever talked to our battalion commander. It's good to talk to you, sir.' The line moved along, and once I got inside I discovered that the officers didn't even have the same dinner hour as the men. They waited until the troops were done, then sat down and got served. I sent for the execs and told him from now on that all officers would eat with the troops."

In 1974 Schwarzkopf was assigned to head the Snowhawks, a force of forty-five hundred soldiers at an Alaskan base. "In the winter they trained to fight as ski troops, in the summer as mountain troops," Schwarzkopf writes. He knew that he couldn't be an effective leader of these soldiers unless he shared their struggles and their hardships: "I figured I'd have to learn fast to have credibility. I hadn't spent any real time in the mountains since my high-school days in Switzerland, and I was a novice at skiing, snowshoeing, and Arctic survival." And so Schwarzkopf took coaching on the fundamentals by "an expert cross-country skier," and he "practiced diligently every day" and had another officer teach him survival techniques. He practiced parachuting because he would be commanding paratroopers: "It was twenty degrees below zero, with a wind-chill factor of minus 120 degrees as I sat in the helicopter's doorway under the wash of the rotor." And when the Snowhawks undertook a seventy-five-mile road march in three days, "My commanders and I trooped along with our men," Schwarzkopf writes. "While the march was arduous for everybody, the sense of unity it produced made it worth every step."

Today, in the civilian realm, the likes of Al Gore and Mark Fields don't need to risk their lives to be great leaders. But they do need to share the struggles, risks, and hardships that they demand of the rest of us. Regrettably, though, most of our would-be "leaders" in politics and business are really the present-day incarnations of those notorious "château generals."

In my own career of two decades as a journalist reporting on America's most prominent business figures, I've found that lamentably few of them share the struggle and risk with their employees. When they do, it's usually in their early, entrepreneurial years as company founders, while they are beginning to build their businesses.

Chuck Schwab shared the struggle when he was running a scrappy start-up. "Whatever needed doing—answering phones, stuffing envelopes, sweeping the floor—Chuck was right there," writes John Kador in his history of the company. It's ironic that the brokerage began an advertising campaign, decades later, with the tagline "Talk to Chuck." In the company's early days, when customers called to trade the stocks in their portfolios, they might actually find themselves talking with Chuck Schwab, the real person, rather than some anonymous representative of the company named for him.

It's characteristic of the brokerage business that things can be quiet for a long while and then, suddenly, it seems as if nearly every customer is calling with orders to buy or sell stocks. So Charles Schwab's headquarters had a traffic light to let Chuck and his other executives know when they needed to help answer the customer service calls. When the light was green, they could stay at their own desks. When it turned yellow, that meant the customer service department had hit capacity. And when it turned red, Chuck and anyone else with a broker's license would run downstairs and work the phone lines.

"Schwab alumni recall those first days as the most heady of their careers. With the founder beside them, they battled an avalanche of orders," writes Kador. "People who lived through those first days came away with an abiding loyalty to Schwab, the company, and a deep affection approaching love for Schwab, the man." The result was that Schwab's people would respond to his leadership as future crises confronted them.

Chuck Schwab's approach echoed the legacy of another great financial innovator who had worked a few blocks away in San Francisco. In 1904, when A. P. Giannini founded the company that became Bank of America, he shared the struggle. Giannini's plan was to serve Italian immigrants in the North Beach neighborhood who had hid their savings as gold coins in their homes. These were people who didn't speak or write English. Other bankers would have shunned their business because they were poor. When these immigrants stepped into Giannini's bank it was usually their first time ever inside any bank. Making them feel welcome and comfortable was the challenge for Giannini's employees, and he made it his own personal challenge. Giannini set up his desk in the open space of the lobby floor, where he had his managers put their desks: "He himself worked there, greeting customers as they entered the bank, answering questions, and often taking a moment or two to socialize," writes

Moira Johnson in her history of the company. "The bank employed Italian-speaking tellers, who filled out deposit slips and loan paperwork for those customers who had not yet learned English. . . . Giannini demanded that the bank's employees follow his lead and treat customers with respect."

While many entrepreneurs act like Giannini and Schwab when they're starting out, it's rare for chief executive officers to continue to share the struggle once their companies become gigantic and wealthy. Wal-Mart founder Sam Walton was that rare exception. Even after he became a billionaire, he followed the same austere expense-account rules for business travel as his employees. Once, when a colleague rented a car for them to share on a trip, Walton made him switch it for a subcompact. "He is not going to be seen in anything better than what his people are allowed, you see," the executive told Walton biographer's Vance Trimble. "Sam Walton is not going to stay in a better hotel than his people are allowed, nor eat in a better restaurant, nor drive a better car."

Sharing the struggle is vital for anyone who aspires to leadership, whether it's the CEO of a company with hundreds of thousands of employees or a front-line manager with less than a dozen people. At Southwest Airlines, for example, the supervisors have always been "player-coaches" who have helped do the work of the ten to twelve front-line workers on their teams, from handling baggage to serving as agents at departure gates. The setup has strengthened the feelings of loyalty coming from the teammates, who appreciate the extra help when they're in a crunch, and it's made the supervisors become better coaches because they understand the work's pressures and challenges firsthand.

Leaders can't fully grasp the situation until they've shared the struggle. "I always believed you can't ask somebody to do a job when you don't know what's involved in it," said Alice Waters, the founder of the legendary Chez Panisse, the most influential restaurant of our time. "Say you're asking somebody to wash dishes. You can't know how hard that is, or what it's really worth, what people should be paid or how it should be set up, unless you experience it yourself."

The "store team leaders" at Whole Foods Markets fall right in the middle between the CEO with thousands of employees and the leader of a small team with a handful: they're the top executives responsible for a couple of hundred workers at a single supermarket. The chain tries to promote a culture of everyone taking responsibility for cleanliness and customer service. Whenever there's a backup of customers waiting at the checkout lines—which often happens at unpredictable times on Saturdays and during the anticipated "rush hour" after church on Sundays—the checkout clerks put out a call for all free hands to come help bag groceries. If at all possible, their colleagues are supposed to hurry over, put on aprons, and help bagging. And that includes the store's "leader."

Darryl was the leader of a Whole Foods in metropolitan Atlanta, and he bagged groceries during the weekend rushes. And he often worked side by side with his people on whatever was necessary at other times. He rounded up shopping carts from the parking lot. He sliced cheeses. He built pyramidal displays of bottles of mineral water. He wrapped plastic bags around loaves of fresh bread. He cleaned up spills in the aisles. And his conspicuous example inspired other people there to join in, such as Emily, who worked as the store's manager for special events and community outreach. "We believe in shared fate," she told me. "If you see a spill on the floor, don't walk by it. What makes a good leader or a bad leader? When you see a team leader get his hands dirty, you will. If they don't, you won't." Emily felt encouraged by Darryl's conspicuous example. She bagged groceries, too. And she helped her colleagues in the seafood department when they needed help giving out samples of crab legs even though she knew that she would stink like fish when she returned home that evening.

When Whole Foods transferred Darryl to become the store team leader in a different state, Emily was disappointed by the new leader in metro Atlanta. "He hibernated behind the desk," she says. And when the new "leader" did make appearances out in the store itself, she thought that he seemed disconnected from what was going on around him and the challenges his people were tackling: "The most important thing is if you're going to be on the floor, be on the floor. Don't half-ass it. But he's on the phone constantly when he's on the floor. I've never seen him build a display. He has his strengths in analyzing the financials, but his weakness is motivating us. The energy in the store is continuing to decrease. Everybody wants to do enough to get by instead of going the extra mile to satisfy and delight the customer and create team-member happiness.

"People don't work for companies, they work for people," she told me. "Before Darryl left, everybody here believed that. I would move for him right now, without a raise, if he asked me to be there. That's what makes a good leader. I didn't realize the impact he had until he left. It's so hard to stay motivated when you have nobody to model yourself on anymore. And I turn it around and say: What does my team say about me if I'm not motivated anymore?"

In his rise to prominence as the top restaurateur in New York City, Danny Meyer shared the struggle with his workers. For the first nine years that the Union Square Cafe was in business, Meyer himself was there every day, and he constantly helped with the most unglamorous aspects of the business: "I would clear and reset tables, check coats, mop up spills, pick up olive pits off the floor, and reset tables along with everyone else. To this day, I can't and won't walk past something dropped on the floor without picking it up. I wanted people to know that this job was neither beneath them nor beneath me."

That's the message that Ray Kroc's actions communicated to his franchisees—the small businesspeople who owned and operated McDonald's stores. When he traveled around the country, Kroc acted as the "self-appointed cleanup man" for the chain: "On his frequent visits to restaurants, Kroc commonly picked up wastepaper on the lot before going inside to see the franchisee," writes John Love in his company history. One of Kroc's executives said: "It was sometimes embarrassing to visit a store and see Ray get out of the car and start picking up the guy's lot. But it demonstrated to the operators that if cleaning the store wasn't beneath the boss, it shouldn't be beneath anyone else."

Unglamorous duties aren't beneath Ellen Sinaiko, the co-owner and manager of La Méditerranée, a small bistro near San Francisco's Market Street. "La Med" has thrived for two decades in one of the nation's most fiercely competitive restaurant markets. The reason for its sustained success isn't simply the food, which is good but not spectacular. It's not the location—even though it's near a busy avenue, scores of restaurants have failed in the immediate neighborhood over the years. And it's not the decor, which is attractive but not nearly as stylish or alluring as many other venues. La Med's success is largely due to the young people who've waited tables there. One of the longtime servers explained to me that they all modeled themselves on Ellen: her upbeat attitude, her unflappable spirit, her easy friendliness and casual efficiency. Ellen asked them all to cover for each other rather than worrying only about their own tables, which is the more natural inclination. She set the example. Even when she was acting as the host or floor manager, she would refill water glasses, bus dishes, or take orders to help out an overburdened colleague. More important, she got to know all of them as individuals and encouraged their creative careers: she attended every one of their dance performances and art exhibits and poetry readings. She bought the handmade jewelry they made. She advised them about romantic troubles and family crises. She introduced them to her husband, Jack, who was an actor, which showed that she understood their mind-set. They knew she cared about them and supported them. Rather than seeing their day jobs as a grind they had to endure to pay the rent, they came to feel like part of a close-knit family of creative artists who bolstered each other. And they worked much harder and better for Ellen than they would for another manager.

Obviously the risks that military leaders must take—risking their lives—aren't demanded of business leaders in normal circumstances. But great risks must be shared in the corporate realm. Reputations must be risked. Jobs must be risked. Money must be risked.

In the early 1960s, when a young man named Warren Buffett recruited backers for one of his first investment partnerships, he knew that he needed to share the risk with the people who entrusted their money to him. He was still an unproven newcomer without a long track record to attest to his abilities. So Warren and his wife, Susie, plunged more than 90 percent of their personal savings into the partnership. So did Warren's assistant, Bill Scott. "It was enormously important to Buffett that his partners see him as trustworthy," writes his biographer Roger Lowenstein. By putting almost all of his own capital at risk, Buffett was able to tell his backers that "we are eating our own cooking." It turned out that what Buffett was beginning to cook was the most spectacular record of any big investor.

Even in the civilian realm, sometimes lives *are* at risk—and leaders find themselves playing an especially crucial role. That was the situation that confronted Urban Meyer when he took over as head coach of the University of Utah's football team in

2003. In early September, the running back Marty Johnson was arrested for the second time for driving under the influence. On Thanksgiving Day, the student began serving a one-month prison sentence. The publicity was damaging, and Meyer faced great pressure from the Utah community to kick Johnson off the team. But Meyer's wife, Shelley, a psychiatric nurse specializing in addiction, persuaded him that this was about more than football: it was about the life of a troubled young man whose addiction could wind up killing him and endangering others as well. So they chose to share Marty Johnson's struggle as though he were part of their own family. Urban and Shelley Meyer visited him in jail. Gigi, their eleven-year-old daughter, wrote him letters. They gave him their emotional support and showed their belief in him. When Johnson was released, the couple helped him get through an alcohol rehabilitation program, and he did his community service. The following season, Johnson rejoined the Utes and rushed for fourteen touchdowns as the team posted an undefeated 12 and 0 record (the best in its history), won the Fiesta Bowl, and finished fourth in the nation in the Associated Press Poll. Johnson remained sober and received his college degree. And Urban Meyer earned an extraordinary reputation for caring deeply about his players. He became the head coach at the University of Florida—and led his new team to the national championship in 2007.

Chapter Five

When You Walk the Walk,
You Gain a Firsthand View

Here's the difference between a good leader and a great one: consider two mayors of New York City, seven decades apart, and how they traveled to the office in the morning.

In January 2002, when Michael Bloomberg began his first term as mayor, he would commute the same way that millions of other New Yorkers did: by foot and by subway. Bloomberg walked the four short blocks from his Upper East Side townhouse to the station at Lexington Avenue and Seventy-seventh Street. He would descend the narrow stairs, swipe his magnetic fare card at the turnstiles, and wait on the platform. Then he would take the No. 6 local train for two stops to the Fifty-ninth Street station, where he would get off, descend another set of stairs or escalators, and wait on yet another platform to switch to the No. 4 express train for the rest of the ride downtown to the City Hall station.

Bloomberg was sharing the struggle and the hardship with his fellow citizens. He, too, contended with the crushing crowds, the uncomfortable temperatures, the occasionally repulsive smells, and the inevitable and infuriating delays: one time he was stranded with hundreds of other commuters on a motionless No. 4 train for a half hour.

When the new mayor "talked the talk," he revealed ambitious goals for reducing the traffic congestion that snarled midtown Manhattan and for cutting the carbon emissions that cause global warming. He encouraged his fellow New Yorkers to take public transportation. By riding the subway every day, he was walking the walk.

Bloomberg's commuting habits were extraordinarily popular with the media and the citizenry. The *New York Times* called him the city's "first subway-riding mayor." *Newsday* lauded him as a "regular Joe Commuter." Bloomberg invited reporters, photographers, and television news crews to come along with him, and they responded enthusiastically. When NBC's news anchor, Brian Williams, rode the No. 4 train with him during the morning rush hour, Bloomberg bragged about how the subway got him around town faster than a sport-utility vehicle. Even though he was a billionaire who could easily afford to hire a full-time chauffeur, Bloomberg seemed to *prefer* the subway.

At least that's how it looked during Bloomberg's first term. But then, during his second term, in the summer of 2007, the *New York Times* found that the mayor was still talking the talk but no longer walking the walk: although he claimed to commute by subway "nearly every day," the reality was that most days he would be driven between his townhouse and City Hall by police officers in a hulking Chevrolet Suburban SUV. The *Times* reporters found that Bloomberg actually took the subway to work only around two days a week. And even then, he no longer walked to his neighborhood station. The SUV picked him up at his front door and whisked him twenty-two blocks to the Fifty-ninth Street station so he could bypass the local train and get right on the express train, simplifying and speeding up his commute.

After the newspaper published its exposé, Bloomberg no longer seemed like a leader sharing the struggle and showing what really mattered through his repeated, consistent actions. He looked like a cynical manipulator who had nearly got away with a publicity stunt. Like the American foot soldiers in World War II, the residents of New York City never failed to detect and despise the false "we."

When Fiorello La Guardia was mayor of New York City, a driver picked him up every morning at eight o'clock. But La Guardia wasn't in a hurry to get to his office at City Hall. He felt an overwhelming need to see firsthand what was happening in his city. In *The Great Mayor: Fiorello La Guardia and the Making of the City of New York,* Alyn Brodsky writes that La Guardia would ask his driver to take detours on the way to City Hall so he could check the progress of snow removal, or gauge how well traffic was moving on the morning rush hour, or see whether the workers were loafing off at one of the government's construction projects. He would get out to talk with police officers about what was happening on their beats, or chat with sanitation workers or even schoolchildren, always curious for details about their lives and what was or wasn't working the way it should. When he saw something that was wrong, he was apt to handle the matter himself right there. Once he personally stopped a taxi for speeding. When a policeman arrived, the mayor shouted, "Get the hell outta here, this is my case."

La Guardia pursued a passionate campaign to take the municipal government, which had been notoriously corrupt under his predecessors, and infuse it with honesty and energy. Whereas other executives might seek refuge in a limousine's backseat to insulate themselves from all the people and the messy reality around them, La Guardia used his chauffeured car as a way of dashing around to see things for himself. He would drop in without warning to make sure that civil servants were doing their jobs correctly.

Once, La Guardia asked his driver to park the car a block away from a government office on the Lower East Side. Then, without calling attention to himself, the mayor walked in and got in the line with people waiting to file for unemployment checks. The line was very slow because some of the clerks were "just hanging out," Brodsky writes. "An enraged La Guardia barreled his way to the front of the line, knocking one attendant back in the crowd, and another who came to the first man's aid. Responding to the commotion, a supervisor sporting a derby hat and with a cigar in his mouth came to investigate. La Guardia knocked the cigar and hat to the ground and shouted, 'Take your hat off, when you speak to a citizen!' It was only then that the supervisor recognized the citizen." La Guardia went to the front of the line, conspicuously took out his watch, and said to the clerks, "Now let me see how fast you can clear up the applicants."

These days we might cringe at La Guardia's physical brusqueness, but we have to admire his fervor for making the city work properly even for the most humble citizens—*especially* for the most humble citizens. Through his daily actions La Guardia showed that there was no mistaking how deeply he cared. By *being there* he was able to see for himself how things really worked—or failed to work—and to push for a multitude of improvements that accumulated over time. One year into the first of his three terms as mayor, the number of grievance letters received at City Hall fell by 90 percent.

Even decades later, La Guardia remained legendary: in 1999, when the top experts in urban politics were polled for the book *The American Mayor: The Best & the Worst Big-City Leaders*, they picked La Guardia as "America's greatest mayor" of all time.

When leaders share the struggle with the rest of us, they earn our trust and loyalty, but they gain even more: sharing the struggle requires the leader to get out there in person among us. And when they walk with us, they see the world through our eyes. They get an invaluable firsthand view of what's happening on the front lines. La Guardia knew exactly what it was like to supervise clerks at an unemployment office or construction workers at a building site or children in a schoolyard, because he saw it all for himself. Simply by taking the subway every day, Bloomberg could glean innumerable insights into the incredibly diverse and complex lives of the people that he was trying to govern. He could sense their moods from their eyes and expressions and energy. He could see what they were reading and how they dressed and what electronic gadgetry they relied on for their news and communications. He could overhear what they talked about. He could see what advertisers were trying to sell them. He could gauge whether problems such as panhandling, vagrancy, and homelessness were rising or falling. And of course he could tell whether the platforms were clean and the trains were running swiftly and the conductors and transit cops and fare-card vendors were being helpful and courteous. Nothing he could read at his desk at City Hall—no report or printout or spreadsheet—could give him this kind of understanding. No table of statistics about subway delays could have the full impact of actually being stranded on the No. 4 train for a half hour.

The firsthand view of the front lines is invaluable. It's what enables the best leaders to stay superbly well informed, freeing them from having to rely on information that comes more slowly and less reliably because it's filtered by intermediaries. It enables them to adjust tactics, develop strategies, sense opportunities, and conceive innovations.

"The general must make himself the eyes of his own army," writes the military historian John Keegan. And the greatest commanders, from Alexander the Great to the Duke of Wellington, did exactly that. Wellington "found no substitute for the evidence of his own eyes." He was a superb horseman and typically rode scores of miles daily so he could see as much as possible firsthand. Before the Battle of Assaye, he rode forty-five miles in a day conducting his own reconnaissance rather than relying on the local guides engaged by his army. Although the guides denied there was a passage through the difficult terrain, Wellington himself discovered a ford that proved crucial to his subsequent victory.

Wellington had a term for his practice of seeing things for himself. He called it "taking trouble." And he was one of its last great practitioners before the advent of the "château generals" of World War I, who never took the trouble. They are immortalized in black-and-white photographs that show them squinting through the lenses of giant telescopes as they make futile efforts to see what is happening at the front, some fifty miles away from their luxurious headquarters in the castles of France and Germany.

In World War II the American generals—including Dwight D. Eisenhower, the supreme commander of the Allied forces—never had a firsthand view of the terrain in France's Normandy region while they were planning D-day, the largest and most complicated invasion in the history of warfare. And so they greatly underestimated the challenges posed by what the Normans called *bocage*—the high hedgerows that were seemingly everywhere. These barriers made it difficult to see the enemy. They confined tanks and trucks to narrow country lanes, blocking them from rolling over the open farmland. This would deny Allied troops the freedom of movement they had counted on.

The problem wasn't that Eisenhower and his aides hadn't been given specific information or prescient advice. Their French allies warned them about *bocage*. British prime minister Winston

Churchill's top military adviser, Sir Alan Brooke, and another one his generals, Sir Frederick Morgan, had traveled in Normandy in 1940 before the Nazis took it over, and they gave the Americans a very accurate description of the terrain and its challenges. "They were very pessimistic about our chances of coping with it," said Lieutenant General Walter Bedell Smith, who was one of Eisenhower's top aides. "But we couldn't believe what we heard. It was beyond our imagination. The fact was that we had to get into the country and be bruised by it before we could really take a measure of it." The Americans needed what the marines call the "ground truth"—the accurate assessment of a battlefield that can only come from seeing it firsthand.

Some of the greatest leadership of the Normandy invasion came not from General Eisenhower but rather from Curtis Culin, the lowly sergeant who salvaged the scrap-metal remnants of the Nazi barricades near the beaches and attached them to the front of his tanks, creating so-called rhinos with "tusks" that could cut through the hedgerows. This shrewd innovation was shown to General Omar Bradley, who spread it to the rest of the American forces. It proved a crucial factor in breaking through the Nazis' defenses.

Fred Smith had been a U.S. Marine, and he understood the importance of "ground truth." In FedEx's early years, he often went at midnight to the company's "hub"—the facility at the Memphis International Airport where incoming airplanes arrived from around the country with cargoes of packages and letters that the employees had to unload, sort, and place on outgoing planes to their proper destinations. The hub had big open portals on all sides to make it easier to move things around. The portals let in the cold air on the winter nights when Fred Smith came to see the action firsthand. Every night was like a crisis—a tremendous amount of work had to be done swiftly and accurately in only three to four hours. To pull it off, FedEx needed strong morale on the front lines. So Fred Smith made sure that all his senior vice presidents shared the struggle: they all spent time working in the hub, loading and unloading packages, especially on the coldest nights, "so they could get the flavor of what the hell was going on," in the words of one of FedEx's managers.

Author Vance Trimble found that Fred Smith walked around the hub at midnight so often that he knew the names of the people who sorted the packages. He also knew all the mechanics, dispatchers, secretaries, and clerks by name, and he listened to what they told him and paid careful attention to what he saw. "Executives were alerted to any detail that contributed to maintaining company morale," Trimble writes. One night at the hub, Fred Smith's second in command, FedEx president Art Bass, noticed that the men's room had run out of paper towels and toilet paper—and no one had cared enough to replace them. "Right then I marched over to the executive offices and had all the towels and toilet paper moved out and put over in the hub," Bass told Trimble. "Then I went in early next morning to listen to our top people complain. One thing about it—it got their attention!"

Like Fred Smith at FedEx, founder Sam Walton at Wal-Mart

was legendary for his desire to see for himself. It wasn't just his famed exploits as an octogenarian piloting his own secondhand propeller plane to barnstorm around the American South visiting four or five Wal-Mart stores a day, walking the aisles and chatting with the clerks. Once he rode shotgun for hundreds of miles in an 18-wheeler Wal-Mart truck to glean ideas about how to improve the company's distribution. Another time he got up at 2:30 a.m. and brought a bag of doughnuts to the employees at a warehouse loading dock to seek their suggestions about how to improve their working conditions. (They asked for more shower stalls, so Sam Walton had them built.) When Wal-Mart was going through its extraordinary expansion across the southern states, Sam Walton didn't hire marketing or demographics experts to tell him where to locate his next stores. Instead he visited small towns himself and watched the traffic going up and down Main Street and around the town square. He had such an instinctive grasp of the "ground truth" that all he needed was to look around a town and he could tell whether a Wal-Mart would succeed there.

While many CEOs and top executives have a practice of occasionally making a "royal visit" to see their workers, or perhaps toiling in a front-line job on a single day a year, for a few hours at most, that's better than nothing but it's not nearly enough. The real difference comes when a leader is obsessive about getting the firsthand view. That's what set apart Fred Smith and Sam Walton. It's what set apart Danny Meyer, who was on the floor of the Union Square Cafe every day for its first nine years as he was turning it into the most popular restaurant in New York

City. And it still sets apart Howard Schulz, who continues to drop in on thirty to forty Starbucks locations every week. When I first met Schulz, in the early '90s, back when Starbucks had only a few hundred locations rather than some fourteen thousand, the man had the strongest coffee breath I had ever encountered. He obviously tasted coffee everywhere he went. He needed to see, and taste, for himself.

When You Walk the Walk, Every Moment Is an Opportunity to Teach, Train, and Lead

When Danny Meyer was a young entrepreneur just starting out in the restaurant business in New York, he found a mentor in the late Pat Cetta, who had enjoyed decades of success running Sparks, one of the city's most celebrated steakhouses. Cetta taught him one of the most important lessons of leadership—and did it through a simple demonstration.

Cetta put a saltshaker in the exact center of a table in the dining room. In the mind of a restaurant entrepreneur pursuing a standard of excellence, that's where it's supposed to be: the exact center of the table. But the harried staffers who set the table will place the saltshaker somewhere near the center but not right in it. They will try to get by with "good enough" rather than striving for excellence. The restaurateur will see this and feel upset, angry, or discouraged, and might respond by yelling at his staffers. But that's not how a leader successfully changes the deep-rooted patterns of how people think, feel, and act. Drawing on his decades of experience of what actually works, Pat Cetta told Danny

Meyer: "Your job is to move the shaker back every time." Not to berate people, assaulting their self-respect. Not to act like the boss and tell someone else to do it.

No, Meyer's job was to do it *himself.*

Is this really the role of the leader? Absolutely. When Danny Meyer stops every time he sees a saltshaker off-center, and takes a moment to reposition it, his people are watching him. His people notice how the leader is walking the walk. And when he does it again and again—not once, not twice, but hundreds or even thousands of times—that's when a real shift takes place: his people begin to act the same way every time. His people come to insist on placing the saltshakers in the exact center of the table. They begin to do it automatically, habitually, without having to take a moment and think consciously about what they're doing. The saltshaker commanding the exact center of the table begins to feel to them, deep in their guts, like the correct way, even the *only* way. When they see an off-center shaker, they'll feel deeply that something is amiss. Their leader has been their model, and they've learned and mastered a new way.

When Alice Waters would see a vase of flowers placed a quarter of an inch off-center on a table at Chez Panisse, her renowned restaurant in Berkeley, California, she wouldn't explode at her staffers. She would simply move the vase to the precise center by herself, knowing that someone would be watching and would learn from her example.

When Fred Smith walked around FedEx's hub operation at the Memphis International Airport, he took the same approach. As one FedEx employee told Smith's biographer: "He is the type of person who would walk into a hangar and see a grease spot and instead of ordering someone else to clean up the spot, he would say 'Pitch me a rag' and he would do it himself . . . He does not vacillate when a problem needs to be solved. He acts."

When Ray Kroc came to visit a McDonald's, he didn't tell his franchise owners to pick up the trash from their parking lots. He did it himself while they looked on.

When you're the head of a company, organization, community, movement, group, or team, everyone is always watching to see how you walk the walk. And so every moment is an opportunity to teach and train. The way that leaders act from moment to moment is part of a long, slow struggle to train their people in many small but vital new habits and behaviors that add up to a fundamentally different way of doing things. It takes a great amount of repetition to change the deep-rooted patterns of how people think, feel, and act. Leaders have to keep moving that saltshaker every day for weeks, or months, or even years. They need to move it hundreds of times, maybe even thousands. They need an exceptional amount of patience and persistence. That's why Danny Meyer calls his approach "constant, gentle pressure," and Bruce Harreld, the senior vice president for strategy and marketing at IBM, who has mentored many of the company's best leaders, talks about the importance of being "boring and relentless."

When you hold the No. 1 position in an organization, every moment is a "teachable moment," whether or not you intend it that way. It's an unforgiving situation. If you act irresponsibly, your personal example confers tacit permission for everyone else to act the same way. If you walk by a table with an off-center salt-shaker, so will your staffers.

Consider this anecdote from Jonathan Schwartz at Sun Microsystems, a major computer company in Silicon Valley. When Schwartz began work at Sun, he was taken out to a long lunch by the chief executive officer, Scott McNealy. Then they returned to the company's headquarters, and McNealy drove them around the parking lot and found that every spot was taken except for the ones right in front of the building's entrance that were reserved for the handicapped and for visiting customers. Schwartz pointed to one of the customer spots and said, "Why don't you park there?" McNealy replied that if he did, then the next day other Sun employees' cars would fill up every one of the convenient spots intended for the visiting customers. That was a lesson that impressed Schwartz—and a story he told me a decade later, after he had become Sun's next chief executive officer.

When I first visited Google's campus in Silicon Valley and saw the beach volleyball court at the center, where employees were playing gleefully in the middle of the workday, I wondered why they felt comfortable with such a conspicuous display of leisure at a company that was struggling to keep up with its extraordinarily rapid growth. A few hours later, when Google's cofounder Sergey Brin walked into a conference room for his interview with me for an article, he was wearing short-shorts, open-toed sandals, and a sweaty T-shirt. For the first half hour, I was distracted by the sight of his hairy legs. He noticed this and apologized for his attire, explaining that he had been playing beach volleyball only a few minutes beforehand. The leader had given his implicit sanction, and that explained why the Google employees weren't afraid of cavorting barefoot in the sand.

When you're the head of an organization or a community, it can be almost comical how your people are apt to imitate you. After General George Custer took to sporting a bright red neckerchief, his stylistic quirk was copied by his staffers, then his officers, and then the enlisted men. The red tie became the sartorial signature of his entire cavalry division. When Bill Gates was running Microsoft in the late '80s and early '90s, he had the habit of rocking back and forth compulsively during meetings. Even though his behavior would have been considered distracting or annoying in other settings, and it was even rumored to be a possible sign of borderline autism, a funny thing happened there: many executives and engineers at Microsoft began rocking back and forth in the distinctive manner of Gates, who was their chief executive officer, their chairman of the board, and their company's cofounder, already a multibillionaire and a legendary figure.

While the wearing of the red tie was an act of intentional imitation by Custer's people, the epidemic of back-and-forth rocking at Microsoft was different: Gates's people didn't even realize that they were doing it. Of course, that's what happens in the process of role modeling. When we admire the head of a team or a community or a company and see them as similar to ourselves in some relevant way, then we learn vicariously from their personal examples, especially when we see their behaviors repeated again and again.

Bill Gates's highly visible and personal example exerted an extraordinary influence at Microsoft, as I saw firsthand when I covered him as a journalist. In 1992, when I was *Fortune* magazine's Silicon Valley correspondent, I set out to write a cover story about Gates. He invited me to sit in as a "fly on the wall" at one of his famous "billg" meetings, an intense four-hour review with the team responsible for one of the company's product lines. (They were named after his e-mail moniker, which is how many colleagues referred to him.) The meeting was fascinating to watch. Many chief executive officers would simply meet with the head of the division, who would meet with the head of the team, who in turn would talk to individual members. Gates pulled them all into one big conference room for an intense, marathon session. This let everyone see how Gates himself reasoned and rebutted. They got a close-up view of how his mind worked. They could absorb his attitude: while many independent observers already saw Microsoft as an overdog matched against weaker rivals, Gates himself thought of his company as a scrappy underdog struggling against tough competitors. Gates's executives and engineers and other employees all saw his restlessness and his complete lack of complacency with the company's already exceptional success. By observing Gates close-up, many people at Microsoft were able to model their own attitudes on his. And so, rather than becoming self-satisfied with their near-monopoly position in operating systems, before long Microsoft's product teams overtook Lotus as the top maker of spreadsheets; dethroned WordPerfect as the leading producer of word-processing programs; and eclipsed Borland as the premier source of computer languages and tools for software developers.

Bill Gates's sometime rival and sometime ally in the personal computer revolution, Steve Jobs, also grasped the power of example. In 1985, after Jobs had left Apple and started his second company, NeXT, he wanted to inspire his cofounders with his passion for aesthetics. He saw an opportunity when they went together to Carnegie Mellon University in Pittsburgh, one of the world's top research centers for computer science, to meet with professors, recruit the best graduate students, and find ideas that they could use for the new company they were conceiving. But then, at the end of the visit, Jobs took them on an unusual day trip. He had arranged for them to drive two hours into the Pennsylvania countryside and spend an entire day on a special private tour of Fallingwater, the architectural masterpiece by Frank Lloyd Wright, the landmark modernistic house of concrete, glass, and steel, cantilevered above a waterfall. They saw that Jobs considered design so important that he couldn't take a routine business trip without making a long detour to find inspiration from the work of a great master.

The realization that every moment is a teachable moment might seem a burden to many executives, but 100 percent leaders see it as a constantly refreshing source of opportunities. Real leaders aren't discouraged by the need to repeat their own personal example again and again, even if few people are around to watch.

Real leaders embrace every chance to influence people, even one employee at a time. What's more, they see every interaction with individuals outside their own organization or movement as an opportunity to win one more customer or convert or compatriot to their cherished cause.

John Chambers, the chief executive officer of Cisco Systems, is that kind of leader. A few years ago, Chambers visited the Wall Street office of James Cramer, who was an influential investment manager at the time. (Since then he has become a popular television personality.) The purpose of the meeting was for Chambers to talk up his stock. But as soon as Chambers entered the office suite, he demanded that Cramer show him the back room where they hid the wiring for their Internet connection. Chambers inspected it and saw that Cramer's firm was using data routers from a rival manufacturer. He demanded that they switch immediately to Cisco's superior product. Then they left the back room and sat down for the meeting. Chambers asked what Cramer wanted to know about the stock. Cramer said that he had just seen all that he needed to see. He realized that Chambers was an intensely driven salesperson who seized every personal interaction as an opportunity to sell even more. That alone convinced Cramer to buy Cisco's shares.

No one exemplified this aspect of leadership better than Robert Mondavi. In the 1960s, when he founded his own winery in California's Napa Valley, the region was known mostly for producing cheap, low-quality jug wines. Mondavi believed that Napa could produce superb wines and become one of the world's greatest wine regions, ranking alongside France's Bordeaux and Burgundy, Italy's Tuscany, and Germany's Mosel. And he had the belief, the determination, and the energy to pursue this extraordinarily ambitious goal, even if it meant having to persuade one customer at a time.

And that's exactly what he did. If he was on a business trip to an American city such as Boston, where it was hard to find California wines on the menus, Mondavi would go out by himself to one of the best restaurants in town and order one or two bottles of France's most expensive and acclaimed wines with his dinner. His order would attract the attention of the restaurant's owner and chef and wine steward. Mondavi would invite them all to his table for a taste of the French wine. Then he would open a bottle from his Napa Valley winery and let them compare it to the best that the French had to offer.

"Sometimes the restaurant owner or sommelier would give me an order right on the spot," Mondavi recalls in his memoir, *Harvest of Joy*. "But even if they didn't, I was never disappointed. I was preaching the gospel as I saw it, introducing them to a new product and a new way of thinking about California wines and the Napa Valley. If they didn't buy now, well, one day they probably would. I knew that what I was really doing, first and foremost, was educating and I knew that process might take time. Most Americans at that time knew next to nothing about fine wines; so I knew I had to be patient. And work like hell."

To Robert Mondavi, every lunch or dinner he ate while traveling was another opportunity to lure potential customers into taste tests, whether they were restaurateurs or chefs or even the other patrons. "I'd order some fine wines and soon I'd have an entire party going on around me!" he writes. When he was back home in Napa, Mondavi would often go out to dinner with his wife, and he would introduce himself to a couple at another table and offer them a free bottle of his wine as his guest: "We generated a lot of excitement like that. And we made a lot of friends, too. Not to mention faithful customers and visitors to the winery."

How many times did Robert Mondavi lure people into trying his wines? Thousands of times, surely, over many years. He had the patience and persistence of a real leader. And by the 1980s, the Napa Valley had become internationally renowned.

Real leaders see everyone they meet not just as a potential customer, but also as a potential compatriot. Jack Welch, the legendary chief of General Electric (GE), always believed that "everyone you meet is another interview." In his memoir he describes an example of how he discovered talented people: "I was in my VW on the New Jersey Turnpike when the engine blew. I got towed to a local garage, where I met a German mechanic, Horst Oburst. Over the course of the next two days, while he was scrambling to get parts, we struck up a relationship. Impressed by his gutsy determination, I offered him a job." Oburst went on to enjoy a successful new career as a plant manager at GE.

Even when leaders are trying to bring change to an entire nation of millions of people, they won't be too haughty to show real concern for one individual at a time—at least not if they're true leaders.

For decades Nelson Mandela recruited his followers one at a time. In 1962, when he went to prison to serve a life sentence, he gave up his belief that South Africa's blacks—who made up 90 percent of the nation's population—could overthrow their oppression by the Afrikaners through violence. Instead he conceived of an incredible new vision: he would attempt to convince the Afrikaners to relinquish their power and follow his leadership as he united the nation peacefully. He aspired to be the leader not only of his own people but of its longtime enemies as well. Today we know that he succeeded, but at the time the idea would have seemed preposterous to anyone other than Mandela himself.

Even though the Robben Island prison colony was harsh and austere, Mandela was allowed to have books, which he used to try to understand the Afrikaners. He taught himself his captors' language (Afrikaans) and tried to learn as much as possible about their history. Mandela had contact with only a few Afrikaners: his prison guards, who were brutish and poorly educated. And so Mandela's efforts to be a leader to South Africa's whites began with his guards. He decided to treat them with respect and dignity, which was exactly what they wanted but had never received, since they occupied the lowliest stratum of white South Africa's social hierarchy. They appreciated the respect. To Mandela, every prison guard represented a valuable opportunity for him to win another supporter and ally—and to learn more about the mind-set and culture of the Afrikaners.

Mandela won over his prison guards, and eventually his prison chiefs. Twenty-three years into his sentence, he was granted a meeting with South Africa's minister of justice, whom he surprised by talking in Afrikaans about Afrikaner history. Later, when Mandela prepared to meet South Africa's chief of intelligence, he learned that the man was a "rugby nut." So Mandela scrambled to learn as much as possible about rugby, the sport of white South Africans. (The blacks played and watched soccer.) He amazed the Afrikaner by talking so knowledgeably about rugby in Afrikaans. Ultimately, Mandela was brought to meet South Africa's head of state, P. W. Botha, who was likewise impressed by the prisoner's command of the Afrikaners' language and history. From starting out one by one with his prison guards, Mandela spent nearly three decades winning the admiration, trust, respect, and confidence of the Afrikaner power structure up to the highest levels. And then, released from jail and elected to office, he won the support of the rest of the nation.

On some occasions, of course, leaders can turn a seemingly routine situation into a dramatic and compelling demonstration that will be witnessed by a large number of people. In 1939, when the Daughters of the American Revolution (DAR) refused to allow Marian Anderson, the African American opera star, to sing at Constitution Hall, their headquarters in Washington, D.C., a segregated city, Eleanor Roosevelt resigned her membership in the organization. That was walking the walk through small steps. But then the First Lady sponsored a free outdoor concert by Anderson on the steps of the Lincoln Memorial on Easter Sunday. Seventy-five thousand people came to the National Mall for the historic event. That was a big step ahead for the civil rights movement. (And four years later, the DAR finally invited Anderson to sing at its hall to a racially mixed audience.)

While big thinking and grand gestures are the stuff of leadership, so are the everyday actions that fewer people see, repeated again and again until they add up. The Napa Valley's reputation received an extraordinary boost when, in 1976 in Paris, its vintages beat the best French wines in a competitive tasting that was judged by leading wine experts and covered by the international media. But even before that event, Bob Mondavi had spent a decade holding countless impromptu wine tastings whenever he went out to restaurants on his travels, and those many encounters inspired the crucial word of mouth that may have been nearly as instrumental in elevating the reputation of California wines. Even for the biggest thinkers, like Mondavi, leadership consists of the smallest actions.

Leaders must have confidence that a seemingly endless number of small steps will take them to their ultimate destination.

You can't *run* the walk.

You have to walk the walk.

Chapter Seven

When You Walk the Walk,
You Take Steps That Every Potential Follower Can Follow

Here are two episodes that show the difference between good leadership and great leadership. They both come from the American civil rights movement.

When Eleanor Roosevelt was First Lady, she attended the Southern Conference on Human Welfare in Birmingham, Alabama, in 1938. It was a gathering of fifteen hundred delegates, both blacks and whites, who opposed segregation. Anticipating trouble from these people, the city's police chief, Eugene "Bull" Connor, vowed to arrest any delegate who broke the state's segregation laws. When Eleanor Roosevelt arrived late on the second day of the conference, she saw that the white delegates were all sitting on one side of the aisle in the hall and the black delegates were all sitting on the other side. She took a seat among the blacks. Then a police officer tapped her shoulder and told her to move.

What should she do? Should she stay there and challenge the officer to arrest her? She was passionate about civil rights, and she wasn't afraid of creating controversy. She had outraged many Americans by "crossing the color line" when a photo was published of her graciously accepting a bouquet of flowers from a five-year-old black girl at the opening of a public housing project. And many years earlier she had been arrested once while taking part in a political demonstration. But now that she was First Lady, her public actions carried extraordinary resonance. And so, at that crucial moment in Birmingham, when her values were tested, she thought quickly and acted creatively: she moved her chair into the aisle between the white and black sections. And she carried her folding chair with her throughout the rest of the four-day conference. She sat in the center of the meeting halls and the churches where the events were held. She said that she "refused to be segregated." The Birmingham police watched her constantly but never arrested her.

For the pioneering activists struggling together in these earliest years of the civil rights movement, Eleanor Roosevelt's gesture of support was highly encouraging. But it wasn't an act of great leadership because they couldn't follow her example. All of the fifteen hundred delegates couldn't move their chairs and sit alone in the central aisle. As soon as one black delegate moved into the aisle alongside the white First Lady, then segregation would have been violated, the law would be clearly broken, and the police could respond.

To be sure, Eleanor Roosevelt's actions in Birmingham were defiant and courageous, and they helped to secure her reputation as the most influential white leader of her time in the cause of civil rights. But for leadership to exert its fullest power, the leader must do what everyone else can follow. If she had been a truly great leader that day, she would have remained in the black section of the hall, challenged Bull Connor's men to arrest her— and called on the other delegates to join her act of civil disobedience. If Eleanor were arrested, every one of those fifteen hundred people could have followed her, and it might have been an explosive event that commanded the attention of the entire world.

Now here's the example of great leadership:

On February 1, 1960, four black freshmen from the Agricultural and Technical College of North Carolina at Greensboro went downtown to Woolworth's and sat at the lunch counter, where all the stools were reserved for whites only. One of the students ordered coffee and doughnuts. He wasn't served, but the four young men lingered at the counter for about a half hour until the store closed. The following morning they came back with a dozen other black students and sat there for several hours, quietly doing their homework and refusing to leave until they received service. The day after, some three hundred joined them, and then, the next day, the turnout reached a full thousand.

The genius of the gesture was that anyone could take their own initiative and do exactly what the Greensboro Four had done, and they could do it just about anytime and anywhere. Within two weeks, the sit-in movement had spread from Greensboro to fourteen other cities in North Carolina, Virginia, Florida, South Carolina, and Tennessee.

The sit-ins inspired stand-ins at movies, kneel-ins at churches, and wade-ins at beaches. By the end of the following year, more than fifty thousand people had taken part in these kinds of demonstrations in more than a hundred places. They succeeded in desegregating lunch counters in dozens of southern cities, including Atlanta. Ralph McGill, the editor of the *Atlanta Constitution,* believed that the sit-ins had a more powerful effect in promoting civil rights than the yearlong boycott of buses in Montgomery, Alabama, led by Martin Luther King Jr., or even the Supreme Court's historic 1954 decision in *Brown v. Board of Education,* calling for desegregation of the schools. "The sit-ins were, without question, productive of the most change," he wrote. "No argument in a court of law could have dramatized the immorality and irrationality of such a custom as did the sit-ins."

The names of the Greensboro Four—Ezell Blair Jr., David Richmond, Joseph McNeil, and Franklin McCain—aren't known to most of us today. But their leadership in 1960 proved more effective than Eleanor Roosevelt's in Birmingham in 1938—or, for that matter, Martin Luther King Jr.'s in Montgomery in 1955. While King coordinated a boycott that ultimately desegregated the buses in one city, the sit-in movement desegregated many public institutions in many cities throughout the southern states.

The Greensboro Four didn't give speeches. They didn't have an organization or a plan. (Even their own initial sit-in was conceived during a conversation late the night before.) But they walked the walk in a way that any potential follower could follow.

That's a crucial lesson that's usually overlooked by our

would-be leaders, especially the ones who have become accustomed to the privileges and prerequisites of position and prestige. Consider Arnold Schwarzenegger, for example. When he ran for governor of California, he said that we needed "strong leadership" to protect the environment, and he promised to reduce air pollution by half in five to eight years. Once elected, he used his political clout to pass extraordinary legislation in 2005 committing the state to cut greenhouse gas emissions 80 percent by the year 2050. Schwarzenegger became one of our foremost figures in talking the talk about energy and the environment.

But he still didn't walk the walk. He continued to own a personal fleet of five Hummers. The hulking, tank-like vehicles were notorious gas-guzzlers (they got only ten miles per gallon, according to *Car and Driver* magazine). What's more, they emitted three times more carbon dioxide than typical cars. In response to public criticism from environmentalists, Schwarzenegger asked General Motors, which owned the brand, to retrofit one of his Hummers to run on hydrogen, and he converted another to run on biofuel. And then he postured triumphantly, as though his Hummers had turned "green."

The reality was that no private citizen could follow his example and drive a hydrogen vehicle. It was an experimental technology that no carmaker had yet put on the market to the general public. And very few people could switch to biodiesel. The supply of diesel vehicles in the used-car market—such as classic Mercedes-Benz cars from the 1970s—was very limited, as were places to buy the alternative fuel, even in California.

Schwarzenegger didn't act in a way that California's thirty-six million other citizens could follow, but when was the last time he had to cope with the constraints faced by the common people? He was acclimated to the privileges of wealth, power, and celebrity. Hummers had been strictly military vehicles before Schwarzenegger first saw them in an army convoy along Interstate 5 in Idaho, when he was filming the comedy *Kindergarten Cop*. The movie star wanted Hummers for himself, so he convinced the manufacturer to come out with a new version for the civilian market. In 1992 he became the first private citizen to own a Hummer, and his endorsements helped the company ramp up its sales to thirty thousand a year. In 2001 Hummer donated $13 million to become a sponsor of the Inner City Games Foundation, which held after-school sports programs for children—and was chaired by Schwarzenegger. Later, as California's governor, when Schwarzenegger faced one of the trade-offs between his competing values, he chose to uphold his loyalty to his longtime financial supporter rather than to share the struggle and sacrifices he was asking the rest of us to make in cutting energy consumption and greenhouse gas emissions.

If Arnold Schwarzenegger had been a 100 percent leader, he would have put on a grand public display of dismantling his five Hummers and recycling the metals and other materials. In their place he could have bought the most fuel-efficient cars on the market at the time. He could also have given up his routine of commuting back and forth by private airplane every weekend between his home in Los Angeles and the state capital in Sacramento. To be sure, it's important for the governor of California to spend a lot of time in and around Los Angeles, which is the state's largest population center. But if he wanted to walk the walk on environmentalism, Schwarzenegger could have chartered a fuel-efficient bus and invited any other state employees to sign up to ride along with him. The bus could have stopped at towns along the way, giving Schwarzenegger more opportunities for a firsthand view of the expansive and diverse state he was governing.

As he strove to recast himself as a leader of the environmental movement, Arnold Schwarzenegger made the same mistake with the vehicles he drove as Al Gore and Laura Turner Seydel did with the houses they lived in. After Gore was lambasted on the Senate floor and in the media for the wastefulness of his Nashville mansion, he rushed to retrofit it with an underground geothermal heating system, rooftop solar panels, and many other costly features that would save energy. Although Gore refused to disclose the amount of money he spent on the remodeling, it was surely in the hundreds of thousands of dollars. That's how much Laura Turner Seydel paid for the architectural features and innovative technologies to reduce the energy consumption of her self-styled EcoManor in Atlanta. The pundit Thomas L. Friedman, who warned about global warming in his best-selling books and his *New York Times* columns, undertook a similarly costly retrofit of his supersized 11,400-square-foot house in the Maryland suburbs of Washington, D.C. Surely Gore, Seydel, and Friedman each dispensed more cash to "environmentalize" their home than the average American family paid for the entire purchase price of theirs.

The Gores, Seydels, and Friedmans are very wealthy people who took actions that could be followed only by other very wealthy people. If they wanted to be real leaders of all Americans, they should have taken actions that the rest of us could afford to follow. All of us who live in large houses can afford to switch to smaller ones when we need to move from city to city for new jobs, for example. People with extra rooms or underused basements or "in-law units" can rent them out to tenants. These might be difficult lifestyle adjustments, of course, and few of us would want to make them unless we had to. That's why we need real leaders to go first, set the example, and share the struggle. Instead we've had ersatz leaders who try to spend their own way out of any situation. That's a solution only in an imaginary world where resources are unlimited.

Chapter Eight

When You Walk the Walk,
You Become a Leader Even Without the
Title, Position, or Formal Authority

In the spring of 2008, a sports agent in Atlanta, Adam Zimmerman, called to tell me about a surprising speech that he had attended. The speaker was a man named Urban Meyer. I had to confess that I didn't recognize the name at all. *Urban?* Who was named Urban, anyway, except for popes of another era? But I was surely in the minority of adult males living in the southern United States who had no idea who he was. Urban Meyer was the head coach of the varsity football team at the University of Florida. Two seasons earlier he had led the Gators to win the title in the South Eastern Conference, or SEC, one of the most competitive leagues in all of college football. Then he led them even further to win the national championship game, enshrining Florida as the undisputed No. 1 among the 117 teams in Division I-A of the National Collegiate Athletic Association. In the southern states, where college football is the only thing that inspires as much passionate fervor and divisive loyalty as religion—where college football is almost a religion in its own right—Urban Meyer is a very big deal indeed. My wife, Susan, who grew up in Atlanta, informed me only half-jokingly that in the South a coach like Meyer is held in a high regard, "just one step below Jesus."

Meyer had visited Atlanta to give a speech to the local UF alumni association. The alumni and boosters were an important constituency. Gator Boosters Inc. raised a stunning $28 million a year, which paid for the scholarships Meyer gave to most of the team's 105 players. Even after chalking up a bunch of outsized expenses—such as Meyer's $3.25 million annual salary, the bonuses he received for winning conference titles and championships, and his use of the university's jet to fly around the country to recruit young athletes—the football team still managed to net millions of dollars for the school from ticket sales and its share of the conference's TV revenues.

The dozens of alumni who gathered for the coach's speech in Atlanta that day thought they knew what he would talk about. They expected Meyer would get them pumped up about the coming season and how Florida would surely vanquish such formidable rivals as Alabama, Georgia, "Ole Miss," Auburn, and Louisiana State. But that's not what the coach focused on. Instead, he spent much of his time describing a recent book that had captured his interest: I was proud to learn that it was a book I had written, *Change or Die*, which explored the psychology of behavioral change. It described the Delancey Street Foundation, which takes heroin-addicted and alcoholic felons out of state prisons and teaches them to live together without drugs, alcohol, threats, or violence. It looked at Dr. Dean Ornish's program, which teaches patients with heart disease to reduce the stress in their lives without relying on smoking, drinking, overeating, or venting rage. And it examined how Toyota took over a General Motors automobile plant, where the workers had fought acrimoniously, and taught them to cooperate in harmonious teams.

It was an unusual move for a college football coach to take such a strong interest in this area of study. The stereotype would suggest that a coach's interest in psychology probably went no further than his trust in common and crude tools such as outbursts and tirades on the practice field and pep talks in the locker room. But Adam Zimmerman, the sports agent, assured me that Meyer was an unusual coach. Meyer had a degree in psychology, as did his wife, Shelley, who worked as a psychiatric nurse. Soon I wanted to meet the legendary figure and discuss his ideas about change and the role that leaders must play. So I drove to Gainesville, Florida, and went to "The Swamp"—the team's ninety-thousand-seat stadium—for a two-hour interview with Meyer on what happened to be his forty-fourth birthday in June 2008.

"Change is what I'm all about," Meyer told me as he sat down in his temporary office, a glass-walled skybox atop the great open concrete bowl of the amphitheater. (He was waiting for construction to be completed on his new office, as part of a $29 million stadium remodeling.) Every season, Meyer explained, he had to take a bunch of teenagers who came from diverse subcultures and get them to live by the code of conduct of the Florida team, which could be dramatically different from what they had grown up with. The situation was the same at major universities everywhere: Some of today's students came from environments where it was commonplace and even accepted for teens to drink alcohol, do drugs, and carry guns, and where boys who got into lovers' quarrels and were hit by their girlfriends would be expected to hit back.

But that way of life had to change once they came to Gainesville and joined the Florida football team. Meyer taught and enforced five "core values": "Honesty, Respect Women, No Alcohol, No Drugs, No Weapons." Once the teenage recruits became Florida Gators, then getting arrested for underage drinking or illicit drugs or domestic violence or on weapons charges could have devastating consequences for them as well as for the team. The incidents would make news in the daily papers throughout Florida and the nightly local TV news and maybe even on ESPN. The news would ricochet through the blogosphere. Transgressing players would be suspended or cut from the team or even expelled from the university, ruining their chances of finishing their college degrees, let alone achieving professional careers in the National Football League. The team would lose valuable players, hurting its spirit and cohesiveness. The team's reputation, and the university's, would be damaged.

Meyer strove to bring about fundamental changes in how his players thought, felt, and acted on the field as well as off. He knew the overwhelming importance of his players being unselfish and supportive of each other on the gridiron. But the pervasive culture of individualism in America promoted selfish play even in the most collaborative of team sports. The stars were the ones who received the attention and adulation. Fans became obsessed with statistical measures of individual performance, which were easy to track and compare. The statistics were especially crucial to how the fans did with their "fantasy football" or "rotisserie baseball" teams, which were make-believe rosters competing in imaginary leagues based on actual stats from real players from assorted real-life teams.

Meyer knew that having star players wasn't nearly enough for a team to win championships. The previous season, he told me, the Gators had played selfishly. They ended the season with a record of 9 wins and 3 losses, and then they lost one more time in the postseason bowl game. While 9 and 4 might sound like a highly respectable record, it was extremely disappointing given the expectations of the team and its community, which had hoped once again to win the conference title and the national championship.

Meyer figured that each season there were only four or five "great teams" out of the 117 teams in Division I-A of the NCAA, and that leadership, not talent alone, was what really made them. The teams played twelve games in the regular season, and Meyer told me: "I think great talent will get you seven wins in this conference. Add discipline, eight or nine. And leadership gets you rings"—championship rings, that is, which start with eleven or even twelve wins during the scheduled slate. Meyer's definition of leadership, in the context of football, was "the ability to respond in a difficult situation and bring others along with you. Can you raise the level of play of people around you? Just because you're a good player doesn't make you a leader."

Leadership isn't limited to the quarterback, who's the center of attention because he takes the ball and initiates and directs the play. Leaders can play on the "special teams," the squads of unsung athletes—their names unknown to the fans watching on television or in the bleachers—that briefly come on the field only for kicks and punts and then return to the sidelines and sit out the rest of the action. "There are guys on special teams who are great leaders—kids respect that and not the great players who can't lead," Meyer said. "We've had example after example of that. One of our best leaders in the national championship was Billy Latsko, a fullback who never carried the ball. Jamalle Cornelius was the team's captain—he was maybe the fourth-best receiver. Everyone respected him so much."

Meyer turned to Latsko and Cornelius at a crucial point in the 2006 SEC title game against Auburn. The Gators were behind 21 to 17, and they were at their own fifteen-yard line facing a fourth down with ten yards to go for a first down. Meyer sent in his special-teams squad, as if the Gators were going to punt, which would be the usual, safe play to call in that situation. But then the punter flicked the ball to Cornelius for a run. Then Latsko provided a crucial block that enabled Cornelius to carry for seventeen yards and a first down. It was a play that they had practiced almost every day for weeks, and they executed it perfectly under great pressure. Even though they weren't the team's greatest athletes, Meyer admired and trusted Cornelius and Latsko so much—for their work ethic and their fighting spirit— that he turned to them to spearhead a risky and unconventional play that Meyer later confessed "could have cost me my job." Meyer's biographer Buddy Martin wrote in *Urban's Way* that it was "one of the gutsiest calls I've seen in four decades of covering football" and "one of the greatest calls" in the team's hundred-year history. The play proved to be the turning point that the players felt had shifted the game's momentum.

I pressed Meyer to estimate how many leaders like that he needed on a team of 105 players. Was it six leaders? Eight? A dozen? Meyer wouldn't specify a number, but he reinforced the idea that it took a number of leaders throughout the different parts of the team. Just to make absolutely sure that I understood him, I said, "Tim is a terrific leader"—referring to Tim Tebow, their six-foot-three-inch, 240-pound quarterback—and wasn't it enough for the quarterback to be a good leader? "No," Meyer said, "not at all."

Intrigued by my conversation with Meyer, I followed the Gators' season that following autumn of 2008. The big story for the team—indeed, the biggest story of the year in all of college football—was the extraordinary performance and leadership of one player: Tim Tebow. The dramatic narrative really began when Florida lost the fourth game of the season by only one point, 31 to 30, to "Ole Miss" (the University of Mississippi). At the televised press conference afterward, Tebow appeared to wipe away a tear below his eye as he delivered an emotional apology and a resolute pledge: "I just want to say one thing to the fans and everybody of Gator Nation: I'm sorry," he began. "Extremely sorry. We wanted an undefeated season; that was my goal, something Florida has never done here. I promise you one thing; a lot of good will come out of this. You will never see any player in the entire country play as hard as I will play the rest of the season. You will never see another player push his team as hard as I will push everybody the rest of the season. You will never see a team play harder than we will the rest of the season. God bless."

Fans of rival teams derided him as "Tear-bow," as if his speech were too unabashedly emotional for the manly stoicism supposedly required of a big-time quarterback. But Tebow fulfilled his promises. The Gators won every game on the rest of the schedule, finishing 11 and 1, a record eclipsed in the conference only by the undefeated University of Alabama, which was ranked as the nation's No. 1 team by the Associated Press sportswriters' poll. In December the two teams met in a postseason game to decide the SEC title. Alabama held a narrow 20-to-17 edge in the second half. But then Tebow led an eleven-play, sixty-two-yard touchdown drive that Meyer later told reporters was "the drive of the year" and "one of the greatest" in the school's history. In a breathtaking fourth-quarter comeback, Tebow guided the Gators to a 31-to-20 victory.

Afterward Meyer said that Tebow had "a special something inside of him, and I'm not talking about throwing and I'm not talking about running. I'm talking about the ability to make the level of play of everyone else around him better." He told the reporters: "My quarterback, I think, is the best in college football. I think he's the best football player in America." *Sports Illustrated* described that special something as "the leadership Tebow exhibited in his tearful mea culpa and vow to work harder after Florida's September loss to Ole Miss; the ability, it seems, to *will* his team to victory."

In December the Heisman Trophy, the annual award for the best player in all of college football, went not to Tebow but instead to the University of Oklahoma's quarterback Sam Bradford, who had even more impressive individual performance statistics, passing for even more yardage and more touchdowns. But the two quarterbacks came head to head in a showdown soon after New Year's, when Florida played Oklahoma in the national championship game. The score remained tied as the fourth quarter began, but then Tebow proved himself anew: somehow, once again, he seemingly *willed* his team to victory. The Gators won by a decisive margin, 24 to 14.

As I watched the championship game, I thought back to the long interview about leadership that I conducted with Meyer before the season began. As I recalled it, Meyer had never even mentioned Tebow by name. Could that have been possible? Was my memory flawed? The previous season, Tebow had been the first sophomore ever to win the Heisman Trophy, and Tebow had a nearly worshipful following among the fans, but Meyer didn't talk about him at all. He talked about Billy Latsko and Jamalle Cornelius.

I looked back through my notebooks, and then listened again to the entirety of the tape recording, and my memory held up. I recalled that Tebow was there that day in Gainesville—he was taping a video segment with the glamorous ESPN correspondent Erin Andrews just outside the stadium where I met Meyer—but the coach made no effort to bring him in to our interview. Why? Meyer was walking the walk. Everything he told me was about the importance not just of one leader but of many leaders on a squad of 105 players. Meyer wanted to talk about leaders I would never read about, never see on the cover of *Sports Illustrated* or the front page of *USA Today*, but who were nonetheless vital to a championship team. In the 2007–08 season, the Gators proved disappointing even with the reigning Heisman Trophy–winner as their quarterback. That hadn't been nearly enough. They needed more leaders, unsung leaders, leaders who might have never carried the ball or scored points but had the ability to carry others along with them as the team responded together to the most difficult situations.

After the Gators won the 2008–09 national championship, I asked one of Meyer's right-hand men about the unsung leaders on this year's team, and found out about three players. They weren't in starring positions—not running backs or wide receivers. Two were on special teams: James Smith, who had handled all the long-snapping duties, and Butch Rowley, who handled all the holding duties. ("Meyer considers him one of the most valuable people on the team and looks to him to get a pulse of the things going on within the team.") And Meyer himself said this about Rowley: "Off the field, he's taught our guys to prepare." The head coach considers special teams so important—a blocked punt or field goal attempt may be the entire difference between winning and losing, for example—that Meyer essentially doubles as the special-teams coach (even though he has a staff of nine assistant coaches).

The third unsung figure was linebacker Ryan Stamper, a leader of the defense. At the beginning of the season, Stamper's teammates voted him one of their captains even though he wasn't slated to be one of the starting players.

Large organizations are much like a 105-player football team in their need for leadership to be distributed throughout rather than coming only from above. In a 2008 cover story for the *Harvard Business Review*, Ed Catmull, the cofounder of Pixar, described the role that leadership played as the animation studio created an unprecedented string of nine blockbuster films, from *Toy Story* in 1995 to *WALL•E* in 2008. Catmull writes that the "creative vision propelling each movie comes from one or two people," the director and producer, who must be given "enormous leeway" by the company. They need to provide enlightened leadership. But making a great movie also depends on leadership throughout the entire large team. "A movie contains literally tens of thousands of ideas," Catmull writes. "They're in the form of every sentence; in the performance of each line; in the design of characters, sets, and backgrounds; in the location of the camera; in the colors; the lighting; the pacing. The director and other creative leaders do not come up with all the ideas on their own; rather, every single member of the 200- to 250-person production group makes suggestions. Creativity must be present at every level of every artistic and technical part of the organization." Just as it's not nearly enough for the Florida Gators to have a quarterback like Tim Tebow, it's not nearly enough for a Pixar film to have a great director, such as John Lasseter or Brad Bird.

A 250-person movie crew needs even more leaders than a 105-person football team. The idea that the director can be the *auteur* (or "author") of a film—a notion that has been popular in academic circles since it was first promulgated by French film critics in the '50s—is patently ridiculous. A film is never "by" one individual (even if that's the grandiose claim made in the opening credits). And yet, without a superb director such as Lasseter or Bird, a project as dauntingly complex and daringly creative and original as a Pixar film, which takes four or five years to create, would never come together so successfully. Catmull writes, "The leaders sort through a mass of ideas to find the ones that fit into a coherent whole—that support the story—which is a very difficult task."

A company or a team or a movement does need "lots of leaders," and those leaders need leaders. But they don't always need to be appointed or given formal titles or authority. Real leaders will emerge throughout the ranks and outside the lines of hierarchy. Anyone who truly walks the walk will set an example for others and ultimately earn their respect and admiration and trust and begin to "bring them along," in the words of Urban Meyer.

The qualities of leadership that Meyer identified for athletes on the gridiron—responding in difficult situations and bringing others with them—are also crucial for soldiers in battle. In his classic study of World War II, *Men Against Fire*, the U.S. military's official combat historian, S. L. A. "Slam" Marshall, wrote that almost always in any company there were a number of privates, who held the lowliest ranking in the military hierarchy, and "whose earlier service had been lusterless, but who became pivots of strength to the entire line when fire and movement were needed, exhibiting all of the enterprise and judgment of good junior leaders. Numerous witnesses attested how the sustained action of these men had rallied others around them." Marshall further observed that "no commander is capable of actual leading of an entire company in combat, that the spread of strength and the great variety of the commander's problems are tougher beyond any one man's compass, and that therefore a part of his problem in combat is to determine which are the moral leaders among his men when under fire, and having found them, give all support and encouragement to their effort."

That's a lesson that Coach Urban Meyer knows well.

Chapter Nine

When You Walk the Walk, You Inspire Belief

No one believed that the awful situation could be any different. It was the early 1980s, and the managers and the workers on the assembly lines at the General Motors factory in Fremont, California, viewed one another with hostility and fear. It was considered GM's worst plant in the United States. Broken beer bottles littered the parking lot. Absenteeism was rampant: on any given day, more than a thousand of the five thousand workers wouldn't show up. The ones who bothered to come to work were distrustful and embittered.

The workers and managers fought incessantly. One of the bitterest of the many battles between the United Auto Workers and GM's management was over the company's push to save money by speeding up the production line. "If you passed out, they dragged your body on and kept the line moving," said Diane Cordero, who put together the steel frames of cars at the Fremont plant. "At GM, controlling the assembly line's speed was a fundamental privilege of management," wrote Paul Ingrassia and

Joseph B. White, who won the 1993 Pulitzer Prize for Beat Reporting for their coverage of the auto industry in the *Wall Street Journal*. "Old-line GM plant managers would sooner pass out hand grenades at the plant gate than allow a laborer to slow down the line."

GM's chiefs believed that they had to control, coerce, and threaten their underlings to get results. "American companies tend, fundamentally, to mistrust workers," wrote Maryann Keller, one of the top analysts of the auto business, in *Rude Awakening*. "There is a pervasive attitude that 'if you give them an inch, they'll take a mile,' because they really don't want to work. The idea, for example, that a worker in a plant would have the power to stop the line in order to eliminate a problem was heresy. Would such permission lead to widespread line-stoppage for every whim?"

Their bosses pushed to speed up the production line, but the workers constantly rebelled. They thought GM was trying to eliminate their jobs by making the work go faster and by replacing them with robots. And they were right: GM's top executives in Detroit blamed the company's problems on its unruly employees. And so GM was investing a stunning $45 billion on automation in order to cut back on human labor.

Tension pervaded GM's plants. Brian Haun, a production supervisor, described the situation for hourly workers: "In the plant, you're treated like a no-mind idiot. You're supposed to come in and just put the parts on the car and shut up and do your job, and if you miss one, I'm going to yell at you, and eventually you get so used to the yelling that it doesn't do any good.

If you're a supervisor, what can you do? You can't fire them—the union won't let you."

At Fremont, the most notorious of the General Motors factories, the managers and the workers clashed over seemingly everything. In 1982 the local union was contesting more than six hundred unresolved grievances. The workers even fought with one another so fiercely that the national headquarters of the United Auto Workers had to seize control of the Fremont branch. GM's vice president for labor relations called the plant's workforce "unmanageable." A large percentage of the workers had been there for twenty to twenty-five years, and they were considered impossibly resistant to change. The situation seemed so hopeless that GM closed down the factory and laid off all five thousand workers.

But then, in an astonishing twist, Toyota came to take them. The Japanese company's motivation was political: in response to the backlash to imports capturing a larger and larger share of the U.S. market, Toyota's leaders wanted to try to make cars with American workers on American soil. So Toyota offered to revive the Fremont plant and produce a GM car there—a Chevrolet. The two companies created a partnership named New United Motor Manufacturing, Inc. (NUMMI). The United Auto Workers said it would go along with the deal so long as Toyota rehired the plant's laid-off workers.

The workers were satisfied about earning paychecks again, but they returned with just as much distrust for their new Japanese bosses as they had for their American ones. The Toyota people said they would create change. Toyota's leaders talked about trusting the workers and treating them with respect instead of hostility and fear. The company's official philosophy was "treating every employee as a manager." But the Americans didn't believe it. In Fremont, one of the union leaders called it "a load of bullshit."

How do you inspire belief? By showing, not telling. So Toyota sent 450 of the U.S. workers to Toyota City in Japan to spend three days at its Takoaka plant. The Americans saw firsthand that Toyota trusted its workers to pull cords or push buttons to stop the assembly lines if they spotted a car with a defect or if they were having a problem. The Americans saw that Toyota actually encouraged its workers to think independently and make their own decisions. They saw that the workers controlled the speed of the production line, not the foremen. There weren't any foremen, actually: Toyota put its assembly workers into small teams of eight to ten people led by fellow hourly workers. The team leaders weren't bosses. They were more like coaches and instructors. The teammates were all trained to do each other's jobs. Instead of having to perform the same boring, mindless, repetitive work, they learned as many as fifteen different jobs. And Toyota trusted the teams to solve most of the problems that arose and to come up with creative ways to make the work easier and save money.

Those 450 American workers returned to California inspired by a belief in a new way of doing things. They became the first team leaders at the Fremont plant, though over time the role rotated and everyone got a chance to be a team leader. The results were extraordinary: absenteeism at the Fremont plant fell from more than 20 percent down to 2 percent. Within three months the workers—free from foremen yelling at them—were producing cars that had hardly any quality defects, while other GM plants routinely had dozens of defects per car. *Consumer Reports* wrote that the Chevy Novas turned out at NUMMI were "a class act among small cars" and had been "assembled, fitted, and finished as well as any Toyota we have ever seen." A *Wall Street Journal* correspondent wrote that NUMMI was producing "some of the best cars that GM had ever sold."

Toyota's leaders had done what seemed unimaginable: they changed the way that the workers thought, felt, and acted. One of the NUMMI laborers, Santos Martinez, said: "I learned a different meaning for the word *respect*—one that doesn't include fear. My responsibility is now to the team, which works together like a family to solve problems and do the job." These same workers had shouted "bullshit" when Toyota's people talked the talk, but now they gushed unabashedly about belonging to a "family" on the factory floor. That's the power of walking the walk. Nothing else inspires such a sense of belief.

Leadership is about creating change, so its greatest challenge comes when change seems nearly impossible—when people feel helpless and their situation appears hopeless. When you talk the talk about change, most people will react with utter disbelief. Unless they have "hope"—defined in the dictionary as "the belief and expectation" of success—they won't summon forth the exceptional energy, tenacity, patience, and persistence they need to bring about fundamental change. Leaders need to inspire that belief through their actions.

In my research about the psychology of change, I've found what I like to call the Four Elements of Belief. The first element is that leaders must believe in themselves. They need a powerful conviction that they are capable of bringing about profound change.

The source of this conviction remains one of the enduring mysteries of human personality. When Nelson Mandela was imprisoned for a life sentence by a brutal regime, what made him believe that he would reemerge—someday, somehow—as the leader who would bring peaceful unity to a nation divided by racial hatred? What made Barack Obama believe that he could overcome the latent racism in America and be elected president?

When I look back at all of the extraordinarily bright and highly motivated classmates I had during my four years as an undergraduate at Princeton, only one of them believed back then that she could change the world—and then went right out and actually did it. She was an almost comically skinny teenager from Texas, and her name was Wendy Kopp. Two decades later, in 2008, she was ranked by *Time* magazine as one of the one hundred most influential people in the world for her leadership of America's educational reform movement. That same year, the editors of Princeton's alumni magazine convened a panel of distinguished historians to rank the twenty-five most influential alumni from throughout the university's 350-year history. Their list included the names of American presidents (James Madison, Woodrow Wilson), literary legends (F. Scott Fitzgerald), and several Nobel Prize–winning scientists and inventors. Even though Princeton had begun coeducation thirty-nine years earlier, the historians selected only one woman for the list: the forty-one-year-old Wendy Kopp from the Class of 1989, whom they ranked as No. 13.

I was a friend of Wendy's when we were in college and worked together on a student magazine. Since then her story has become legendary: how she set forth her plan for Teach for America in her senior thesis—her extraordinarily ambitious vision of recruiting the nation's top college graduates to spend their next two years as teachers in some of the nation's most troubled public schools in the most impoverished communities in inner cities and rural outposts.

We know now that Wendy Kopp succeeded brilliantly: Teach for America has become a powerful force. By 2008 it had placed seventeen thousand teachers in the schools. That year the program received a stunning twenty-five thousand applicants for its thirty-seven hundred positions. Kopp's nonprofit organization ranked alongside high-paying Wall Street investment banks such as Goldman Sachs and prestigious consulting firms such as McKinsey & Company as one of the ten most sought-after employers of graduates from the highest-ranking colleges. A study found that three-quarters of school principals believed that Teach for America's teachers were more effective than other teachers. Teach for America's alumni have gone on to found national chains of charter schools (such as the extraordinarily successful Knowledge Is Power Program, or KIPP) and to assume important public positions (such as superintendent of schools in Washington, D.C.).

Kopp didn't come from a family background of great wealth or power or celebrity. What made her believe that she was capable of changing the world? What made her think that she could spearhead a movement to confront the educational crisis in America, one of the nation's seemingly most intractable problems? Even though she received an A from her thesis adviser at Princeton, the professor also called her "quite evidently deranged." To any reasonable person, that's how the twenty-one-year-old Wendy Kopp might have appeared when she talked about her vision. She announced her intention to do something that seemed nearly impossible. And then she did it.

That ineffable quality that Wendy Kopp possessed, even when she was twenty-one, is exactly what Teach for America tries to instill in the twenty-two-year-olds it hires. Recently, when I interviewed Kopp at her office in Manhattan, she explained the situation this way: Imagine a troubled school in New York City's borough of the Bronx. Two classrooms, side by side. Each one has a teacher from Kopp's program—someone who's youthful, energetic, smart, highly motivated, and has gone through the same training at TFA's summer workshop between finishing college and starting their first year teaching in the program. The two teachers have résumés that look nearly identical. They're assigned classes where the students are several years behind the expectation for their grade level. In the first classroom, you would see "a valiantly committed teacher who is trying to get the kids to sit in their seats." But in the second classroom, the other teacher has somehow gotten the kids to act as though they're "on a mission"—working extremely hard and making an astonishing four years' worth of academic progress in only nine months.

What's the difference between these two teachers? The first one will feel blocked by the formidable barriers of the situation. He will feel frustrated that there aren't enough hours in the school day to take fifth graders stuck at the first-grade level and catch them up to the sixth-grade level. But the other teacher will surmount the obstacles. He will find some ingenious way to get the students to come in early and stay late—perhaps by telling the pupils "that they were specially placed in his classroom on a top-secret mission to achieve academically because of their high potential for success," Kopp says.

The basic difference between the two teachers comes down to their belief in themselves—whether or not they have the conviction that they can triumph over whatever confronts them. Whether or not they accept limits to what they can achieve. Whether they view intimidating obstacles as legitimate excuses for failure—or whether they think that somehow, some way, they can overcome anything. Whether they "face inevitable challenges with resourcefulness and relentlessness," in Kopp's words. Whether they have what academic psychologists would call a very high "internal locus of control."

"We have spent a lot of time trying to understand what the most successful teachers do in this context," Kopp told me in our interview. "They operate the same way as successful leaders in any other context. Teaching is leadership. At some level Teach for America is teacher training, but it's really leadership training: getting people into the mind-set of really recognizing their control over the situation."

It all starts with leaders believing in themselves, but that's not nearly enough. Leaders need to believe their people are capable of profound change. That's the Second Element of Belief, and it's a terrible stumbling block for many elites as they try to become leaders. The intelligent and energetic people who have graduated from the top colleges and universities and gone on to positions of power and responsibility are very confident of their own abilities, but they don't necessarily believe in the potential of the rest of us. The honchos at General Motors didn't think that unionized hourly workers were capable of working hard, making their own decisions, and being responsible and accountable. But Toyota's leaders believed it. The teachers and principals and superintendents in the most impoverished inner-city and rural school districts didn't believe that most of their pupils could succeed. But Wendy Kopp believed it, and so did her corps of teachers.

The leaders' conviction must inspire the leaders' actions. By how they walk the walk, leaders need to show that they believe in their people. That's the Third Element of Belief.

And it's done brilliantly at KIPP, the charter schools founded by Teach for America alumni Mike Feinberg and Dave Levin. Before enrolling at KIPP, many of the students—who mostly come from families with low incomes and qualify for the free-lunch program—had never known anyone who had gone to college. Their parents and teachers didn't expect that they would go and didn't hold that up as an aspiration. And the students had average reading and math scores at only the 28th percentile nationally, putting them way behind most of their peers. But in many cases their first contact with KIPP revolved around the astonishing notion that they could actually go to college. When KIPP was getting ready to open its first middle school in San Francisco, the teachers went to the parking lots of shopping malls to recruit students with that very pitch.

When students begin the fifth grade—the lowest rung at KIPP's middle schools— they're typically ten years old, which is eight years away from when they can enter college and twelve years away from when they would likely graduate. But their fifth-grade class is identified by the year that those students will graduate from universities. If you entered KIPP as a fifth grader in the fall of 2009, then you would constantly hear the teachers and principal talk about you and your classmates as belonging to "the class of 2021" instead of calling you "the fifth grade." Your classroom would be named after the university attended by your teacher—"Harvard," for example, or "Stanford," or "the University of California," which are the kinds of places you're expected to get into.

KIPP's teachers show their sincere belief in the students, which inspires the students' hopes for going to college and motivates the exceptional commitment of time and energy that the children need to put into their studies. KIPP schools typically run from 7:00 a.m. to 5:00 p.m. on weekdays, and the "Kipsters" have to attend classes for four hours on Saturdays as well as for a month during what used to be their summer vacations. They spend 1,878 hours a year in school, which is 62 percent longer than the average of 1,170 hours that their peers spend in the city-run schools in the same neighborhoods.

The teachers don't just talk the talk about how important it is for their pupils to excel and go on to college. They walk the walk by sacrificing much of their own personal lives to make it happen. Not only do the teachers spend much more time in the classroom than their city-school counterparts, but they also give out their cell phone numbers so students can call in the evenings with questions about homework. That extraordinary access shows that the teachers have a deep commitment to the success of the students, and it helps to transform the relationship and infuse it with intense emotional power.

By the time the Kipsters are ready to graduate from the eighth grade, their reading and math scores have risen dramatically from the 28th percentile to the 74th percentile, which ranks them ahead of many of America's more affluent school districts. That's simply a fantastic achievement. Typically, KIPP's eighth-grade graduates go on to attend outstanding magnet public high schools, which serve the best students from around their city, or they receive scholarships to attend the most prestigious private high schools, including such elite institutions as Exeter and Andover. Their KIPP education makes them twice as likely to go to college. In Houston and New York, the two cities where

KIPP first opened schools, only 48 percent of the public high school seniors go to college; in comparison, 80 percent of the Kipsters have been accepted to college. It's no wonder the *Washington Post* wrote that "KIPP appears to be the most interesting and successful attempt so far to raise the achievements of low-income, minority children."

The Fourth Element of Belief is that leaders must get their people to believe in themselves—to expect that they can and will accomplish a profound and positive change. In many ways this is the hardest challenge of all. I've found that it's best accomplished by a certain kind of role modeling: before people believe in themselves, they need to see other people just like them who've overcome the same obstacles and achieved the same change.

This is one of the powerful ideas behind an extraordinary program called the Delancey Street Foundation, which takes heroin-addicted and alcoholic felons out of the state prison system and has them live together in a waterfront complex in San Francisco that looks like an expensive condominium rather than a halfway house or rehab center. The site has five hundred residents, and only one of them isn't a former addict or ex-con: she's the program's cofounder, Mimi Silbert, a tiny sixty-seven-year-old grandmother who holds doctorates in both psychology and criminology. While the established wisdom in her field claimed that prison inmates were typically "psychopaths" who had no empathy for other people and were incapable of changing, Silbert believed that they could learn to live without drugs, alcohol, threats, or violence, and then reenter the mainstream society as peaceful, prosperous citizens. She has shown this belief by living among them—she's been a resident at Delancey Street for thirty-eight years, ever since she started the program in 1971, and she raised her two sons there among the former pimps and prostitutes and gang members and drug lords. She made herself vulnerable to some of society's most violent and lawless members in the belief that they could live together like a family. In my two decades as a reporter, I've never seen a more inspiring example of walking the walk.

Although Silbert knows that addicts and felons are capable of fundamental change, the addicts and felons don't start out believing it. Not at all. They come to Delancey because judges offer the program as an alternative to yet another prison sentence. At first, many of these repeat offenders see Delancey as a "get out of jail free" pass. Thinking with a criminal's mentality, they view Delancey as a scam that they're shrewdly exploiting. Instead of submitting to prison guards or parole officers who love to "kick their butts," they're scheming to get away with "one more con" by taking advantage of San Francisco liberals who like to "kiss their butts." They don't go to Delancey believing or expecting that they can change how they have always lived. Deborah, for example, was a heroin addict at twelve and a street prostitute at thirteen. She dropped out of the ninth grade. Her baby drowned in the bathtub while she was getting her heroin fix. She spent five years in prison. She went through many programs and hospitals, playing what she called "the cure game," but she knew that she would always be an addict. She tried to kill herself three times. Then, "to beat a prison case," she went to Delancey.

The new residents at Delancey have long believed that the only way for people like themselves to become powerful and prosperous is by dealing illegal drugs, so some convince themselves that Delancey must be a scam, an elaborate cover for a drug operation. Deborah stayed at Delancey because she believed "there must be something 'dirty' going on," and she wanted to get in on the action. Of course there's nothing dirty going on. Instead the newcomers see the longer-time residents who have lived there without drugs, alcohol, threats, or violence while they're working in the businesses that Delancey Street runs to support itself: a house-moving service, a waterfront restaurant, a bookstore-café, a Christmas tree sales operation, and a print shop. Instead of profiting as gang leaders or drug dealers, they're helping to bring in millions of dollars in revenues as managers of the moving business or as chefs and servers at the restaurant. And ultimately the newcomers begin to think that they, too, can be like Delancey's veterans. Their disbelief turns into belief and then into the hard work needed to make the change. When they've seen people just like them walking the walk, they know that they can walk it, too.

Delancey Street has a powerful, self-perpetuating culture, but it only came about because of the extraordinary work of a leader who embraced the Four Elements of Belief.

"To get the culture started, you have to believe in it, live it, show it, be part of it," Mimi Silbert once told me. "You have to be willing to jump in a hole with people. The leader has to be willing to do it *with* people. 'Change' was a verb and it should stay a verb. It has to happen in *action*. You have to *do it*. I don't think a leader can accomplish major change without being willing to slice yourself open and become part of the change."

In my view Mimi Silbert and Wendy Kopp both point toward the wisest and most concise formulations of what leadership is all about. While "change" is a verb, "lead" is a verb, too. You have to *do it*. And while "teaching is leadership," as Kopp says, the reverse is equally true: "Leadership is teaching." That's the essence of how leaders act.

This is what we have a right to expect of the people who aspire to be our leaders: through their actions they must show us what's most important. They must be there with us to share the struggle and the risks and the hardships. They must see for themselves what we are seeing. We will always be watching what they do, so they must seize every moment as an opportunity to teach us. They must act in ways that we can emulate. And they must show us that we are capable of accomplishing far more than we ever believed.

When the great Jewish religious scholar Hillel was once challenged to explain the Five Books of Moses—the full Torah—while standing on one foot, he responded brilliantly by stating the Golden Rule: "What is hateful to yourself, do not do to your fellow man." Leadership can be explained just as succinctly. Ultimately, it doesn't depend on who you are or even what you say or how you say it, but only on what you do. Although leadership is very difficult, it is also breathtakingly simple: it all depends on how you walk the walk.

The "Walk-the-Walk" Personality

When I began researching this book, I would have agreed emphatically with the great business writer Peter Drucker's argument that there was no such thing as a "leadership personality." In an influential 1988 article for the *Wall Street Journal*, Drucker gave this example: "Franklin D. Roosevelt, Winston Churchill, George Marshall, Dwight Eisenhower, Bernard Montgomery and Douglas MacArthur were all highly effective—and highly visible—leaders during World War II. No two of them shared any 'personality traits' or any 'qualities.'" And as for that inexplicable quality of "charisma," which was widely thought to be the most important trait for people who aspire to create change in organizations, cultures, and nations, Drucker wrote that "Dwight Eisenhower, George Marshall and Harry Truman were singularly effective leaders yet none possessed any more charisma than a dead mackerel."

Over the past two decades my own work as a journalist has given me the chance to get to know many of the most prominent business leaders of our time, and I've also found that their personalities are remarkably diverse.

Consider, for example, the contrasts between two of the most influential figures in the technology field: Steve Jobs and Bill Gates. Soon after *Fortune* sent me from New York to San Francisco in the early '90s to become the magazine's Silicon Valley correspondent, I did face-to-face interviews with each of these legendary figures. I can still recall my first encounter with Apple's charismatic cofounder with startling clarity. It influenced this passage from my 2000 book, *The Second Coming of Steve Jobs*:

> It's easy to understand why reporters fell for Steve Jobs. He was *seductive*, that was the most accurate word for it. When he was trying to woo a person—a reporter new on the beat, an executive he wanted to hire for a job, a potential customer, a strategic partner looking to make a deal—he could be extraordinarily charming. He had the kind of rare hypnotic eyes that are perhaps the most essential quality of a Hollywood star. If you were meeting him for the first time, he would look at you eye-to-eye with a searching, unyielding, laser-like stare. He would say your first name, say it often, insert it casually at the beginning or end of a sentence. . . . Even more important than the substance of what Steve said was the compelling way that he said it. His enthusiasm was carried by the rhythms and tones of his speech. It was the kind of verbal gift that belonged to the most persuasive politicians and evangelists. JFK had it. So did Billy Graham. It

was powerful and infectious. You met him and listened to him and then you wanted to be around him as much as you possibly could.

When I went to Seattle to interview Bill Gates for a *Fortune* cover story about Microsoft, there was nothing seductive about the software entrepreneur. He made no effort to woo me. He was not charming. He avoided eye contact. I would have been surprised if he had made any effort to remember my name. Everything about his vocal tone and his body language signaled that he didn't really want to be participating in the interview. He was visibly bored with having to answer the kinds of questions that a reporter for a popular business magazine needed to ask, and he responded in such a lackluster way that I became nervous about whether I'd wind up with the minimum of quotable material that I needed for the story. He acted as though the situation wasn't sufficiently interesting to him intellectually to merit his attention, and he seemed resentful about being taken away from what he obviously regarded as his more meaningful and important work.

It was obvious that Gates assumed that I wasn't smart enough to be worthy of his engagement and that the burden fell entirely upon me to prove otherwise. Toward the end of the hour-long time slot set aside for the interview, I realized that I would have to be the one to find some way to woo *him*. I would have to make him want to talk with me again. Abruptly I discarded my planned questions about Microsoft's business and the technology industry and chatted instead about one of Gates's heroes, the legendary physicist Richard Feynman. I mentioned that I was writing a book review about a new biography of the Nobel Prize winner, and it turned out that Gates had acquired a set of many hours of unpublished videotapes of Feynman's physics lectures at Cornell University. When Gates saw that I was knowledgeable about Feynman, he offered to lend me those tapes—and I knew that I had broken through a barrier.

My first encounters with both Gates and Jobs suggest just the beginning of the problems of trying to study a "leadership personality." Here were two exceptional leaders in the same industry at the same time, and they seemed to be opposites in so many ways.

The whole question of whether there's a "leadership personality" is further complicated by the fact that personality isn't fixed and permanent. While any parent can tell you that children have distinct personalities from infancy, it's equally obvious that people change over time—and sometimes they change dramatically. That's true even for the most strong-willed business leaders. When I interviewed close friends and colleagues of both Steve Jobs and Bill Gates, I found out that each man had openly envied the other: Jobs was widely seen as a true visionary but he yearned for recognition as a great businessman. Gates was credited with being a great businessman but he wanted to be known as a true visionary. Those desires drove each of them to change remarkably as their careers progressed through the late 1990s and early 2000s. When Jobs returned from a decade-long exile to lead Apple Computer for the second time, he did more than mastermind the design and promotion of startlingly original products. He surprised his critics with his newfound mastery of the mundane but crucial aspects of running a major corporation, such as inventory management. Gates ultimately earned a new reputation as a visionary when he became the world's biggest and most influential philanthropist and brought an innovative approach to addressing major global health problems. Back in the early '90s, no one would have guessed that Steve Jobs, who had viewed himself as an artist, would ever be interested in supply-chain efficiencies, or that Bill Gates, once an icon for greed and ruthlessness, would be extolled for generosity and public-spiritedness.

But there's yet another complication to this whole issue of whether there's a "leadership personality": many CEOs and other heads of organizations or movements or teams combine certain elements of leadership with some aspects of rulership or stewardship. Bill Gates was both a leader to his employees at Microsoft, getting them to adopt an underdog mentality that avoided complacency with the company's success, and he also acted as a ruler of the software industry, as evidenced by the company's expensive settlement with the Justice Department over its strong-armed, monopolistic practices. During Steve Jobs's first tenure at Apple he was a leader who got people to think in new ways about technology, but during his second tenure there he also became an effective manager who made his company's prosaic operations much more efficient.

But having made all these disclaimers in advance about the complications and pitfalls of discussing the "leadership personality," I've eventually come around to thinking that such a thing does indeed exist. To walk the walk, and to keep on walking it, demands certain traits—or, in many cases, it builds up those traits through the active practice of real leadership. And those basic qualities should be clear from the examples portrayed in this book.

Chapters 1, 2, and 3 show that leaders must have exceptional *focus*, always acting to highlight the one or two things that are overwhelmingly important to the cause—the first virtues, or the Rule of One or Two.

Chapters 4 and 5 show how leadership depends on *empathy*. Leaders need to understand and be sensitive to the thoughts, feelings, and experiences of the people they're trying to lead. And there's no better way to develop this trait than by actually sharing the struggle and risk with their people and seeing it firsthand from out in the field.

Chapter 6 shows how real leaders need *constancy* (or maybe a better word is *relentlessness*) because everyone is always watching to see how they walk the walk, and since every moment is an opportunity to teach, train, and lead.

Chapter 9 shows that leaders have an extraordinary *belief* in their own ability to overcome obstacles as well as the potential for their people to change dramatically.

But I think that perhaps the most overlooked personality trait of leaders who walk the walk is what enables them to keep walking it. Call this *persistence, tenacity, resilience,* or *endurance.* I began this book by defining leaders as people who strive to change the ways that others think, feel, and act, and that kind of transformation, especially among a large group of people, takes considerable time and constantly repeated actions. IBM's senior vice president for strategy and marketing, Bruce Harreld, got it exactly right when he said that leaders must be "boring and relentless." That's what it takes to keep doing the same thing over and over again until it really sticks—and then do it some more. While we prefer to glamorize the qualities that we seek in our leaders, rhapsodizing about "charisma" or "vision" or "genius," we often overlook the value of personas that don't seem exciting at all: being so extraordinarily focused as to seem one-dimensional or boring or what Amazon.com's Jeff Bezos likes to call "simpleminded."

Even Steve Jobs, who perhaps more than any other business leader of our era has been hailed for his charisma, vision, and genius, owes his success to his exceptional persistence and tenacity. The first virtues that Jobs instilled in Apple's culture could be called "design" and "originality." But to "think different" (in the words of Apple's famed slogan) means to take outsized risks as a matter of course. In the pursuit of these values, Jobs has inevitably hatched as many flops over the past four decades as he has produced hits. The Apple I was a small seller, but the Apple II was a sensation. The Lisa computer bombed, but the Macintosh, after a slow start, became an enduring success. During his long exile from Apple, Jobs nearly lost his entire personal fortune betting tens of millions of dollars on two start-up companies that struggled for a decade: NeXT Computer was a high-profile failure, but Pixar ultimately made him a billionaire and revolutionized the field of motion picture animation. During his second tenure at Apple, Jobs had some conspicuous nonstarters (does anyone even remember the Mac Cube or Apple TV?) along with his blockbusters (the iMac, iPod, iTunes, and iPhone).

In 2008, when Jobs appeared alarmingly gaunt and sickly during his public appearances, sparking rumors that he was suffering from a relapse of pancreatic cancer, I was often called by reporters who were writing articles speculating on whether Apple could find a successor who would continue the remarkable success of Jobs's run. Could the board tap another leader from within Apple, or from elsewhere in Silicon Valley or even further afield in American business, who possessed the same kind of charisma and vision and genius?

Reflecting on the question, I responded that the real problem would be finding someone with Jobs's extraordinary persistence, resilience, and tenacity—his *staying power,* his ability to walk the walk and then keep on walking it.

The final proof of leadership isn't having new ideas; it's pursuing an idea obsessively—with every action, in every moment, with everyone watching—for many years or even for several decades. That's when you're a real leader.

A Week of Walking the Walk

Everyone is always watching a leader, and never more so than when he's the leader of the world's most powerful nation, and never more so than when he represents a historic change, and never more so than when he has to confront the worst economic crisis in a generation, and never more so than when he begins his first week in power.

At 8:28 a.m. on Wednesday, January 21, 2009, when Barack Obama arrived for work at the West Wing of the White House, it had been nearly two years since he had launched his campaign. He had set forth his ideas and ideals in countless speeches and interviews. He had proved his oratorical brilliance on many occasions, including the day before in his inaugural address to a record crowd of 1.8 million people. That night he didn't get back to the White House until 12:55 a.m., after dancing with Michelle at all ten inaugural balls. He probably slept for less than four hours, since vigilant reporters noticed the lights going on at the White House's private residence at 5:00 a.m. Later that morning, as he began his first full day as president by spending ten minutes alone in the Oval Office, he finally faced the truest and toughest test of any leader: after two years of his talking the talk—constantly, consistently, and often brilliantly—the world would finally see how he walked the walk. What he actually did in his first days in office would show what he considered most important.

Would it be the economy? Or the war in Iraq? Or health care? Those had been the top three priorities, in order, that he had specified again and again during the campaign. He would begin to address all three during his first partial week in office. He would hold a closed-door meeting with Republican leaders from Capitol Hill about his economic stimulus legislation, which included provisions for extending health benefits for displaced workers. He would summon his military chiefs to the White House and direct them to come up with plans for ending the Iraq War responsibly within sixteen months.

But neither the economy nor the war nor health care would emerge from those earliest days as what Obama signaled was most important to his presidency. His Rule of One or Two, expressed in his flurry of executive orders and directives during his first seventy-two hours in office, was about rolling back George W. Bush's unprecedented expansion of presidential power. Bush had often acted as though his power were unlimited, unchecked, and unaccountable. He refused to abide by international treaties his nation had signed, such as the Geneva Convention against the torture of prisoners of war. He often openly refused to carry out his duties to enforce legislation that

Congress had passed—even when he was the one who signed the bills into law—and he directed federal officials to operate under a cloak of secrecy that obscured violations of civil liberties as well as acts of profiteering.

The Constitution calls for the president to "take care that the laws be faithfully executed," but Bush acted as though he were a law unto himself. In 2006 the *Boston Globe* wrote that "President Bush has quietly claimed the authority to disobey more than 750 laws enacted since he took office, asserting that he has the power to set aside any statute passed by Congress. . . ." The veteran political journalist Elizabeth Drew wrote in the *New York Review of Books:* "During the presidency of George W. Bush, the White House has made an unprecedented reach for power. It has systematically attempted to defy, control, or threaten the institutions that could challenge it: Congress, the courts, and the press." She added: "Bush has time and again said that he feels free to carry out a law as he sees fit, not as Congress wrote it. Through secrecy and contemptuous treatment of Congress, the Bush White House has made the executive branch less accountable than at any time in modern American history . . . This power grab has received little attention because it has been carried out largely in obscurity."

Obama's first priorities—even more urgent than reviving the troubled economy—were to restore the strict limits to executive power envisioned by the nation's founders: the Constitution, the rule of law, and the checks and balances of an open democracy. On his first full day in office, Obama—who had once been a teacher of constitutional law—proclaimed unambiguously: "Transparency and the rule of law will be the touchstones of this presidency." Those would be his No. 1 and No. 2 virtues.

And so Obama began his presidency by suspending the military tribunals at Guantanamo Bay, which had held suspects for years without charging them with crimes. The tribunals were, in the words of a *New York Times* editorial, "a mockery of American standards of justice and due process." He ordered the closing of the Guantanamo Bay Detention Camp as well as the Central Intelligence Agency's secret prisons around the world. He banned torture from military interrogations. He ordered that former presidents and vice presidents make public the sensitive documents from their time in office. He instituted the toughest ethics rules of any administration, closing the so-called revolving door that had enabled lobbyists to become government officials and then profit when they left office by lobbying their former colleagues. He directed federal officials to be dramatically more responsive to Freedom of Information Act requests that revealed the inner workings of government. And he instructed the Department of Transportation to begin implementing a law, passed in 2007, that required the automakers to make cars and light trucks with 40 percent higher gas mileage by 2020—one of those hundreds of laws that Bush had refused to enforce.

Bush's defiance of Congress had been especially fierce when it came to laws governing the military and intelligence operations. In his first minutes in office, during his inaugural address, Obama said, "We reject as false the choice between our safety and our ideals." His words were a rebuke not only to Bush, who seemed visibly uncomfortable as he listened a few feet away, but also to many other wartime presidents who had seized extraordinary powers on the assertion that the demands of security could temporarily trump the constitutional protections of liberty. Franklin Delano Roosevelt, in his State of the Union address in 1943, declared America's support for the "Four Freedoms" around the globe—freedom of speech and expression, freedom of religion, freedom from want, and freedom from fear. He denied the most basic freedoms of Japanese Americans by forcing them into internment camps. Woodrow Wilson declared that America was fighting in World War I to make the world "safe for democracy" while he infringed liberties at home by imprisoning or deporting the critics of the war. Even Obama's own hero, Abraham Lincoln, on whose Bible he put his left hand while taking the oath of office—had suspended *habeas corpus* during the Civil War. And so Obama's clear statement—that our founding ideals of liberty must remain inviolate even during threats to our national security—marked a historic shift, and he followed his speech with swift and decisive action to show that he meant it.

Would he stick by this tough choice, this Rule of One or Two, through four (or eight) years of presidency? His predecessors, for the most part, had lamentable records of walking their walks. Bill Clinton began his first term proclaiming that health-care reform would be his highest priority. But then he doomed the initiative when he invested too much of his crucial political "capital" in making deals on Capitol Hill to pass the North American Free Trade Agreement (NAFTA) instead. John F. Kennedy said in his inaugural address that America would "pay any price and bear any burden" in the fight for freedom around the world, but then he opted for an on-the-cheap attempt to liberate Cuba: the Bay of Pigs invasion, which proved disastrous. Dwight D. Eisenhower took the oath to uphold the Constitution and the nation's laws, but he was so slow to enforce the Supreme Court's *Brown v. Board of Education* ruling on school integration that even Stephen Ambrose, his generally admiring biographer, wrote: "With regard to civil rights . . . Eisenhower's refusal to lead was almost criminal."

To be sure, a few American presidents have truly walked the walk, upholding their highest values despite the extraordinary costs and consequences. George Washington was deeply troubled by the institution of slavery but believed that it had to be accepted in order to maintain the union, his highest value for his new nation. Lyndon Johnson spent his political capital passing historic civil rights legislation even though he knew that the backlash would be devastating for the Democratic Party's prospects for a generation.

In his first seventy-two hours as president, Obama showed an intuitive grasp of leadership. On Wednesday, January 21, his first full day in office, he ordered a salary freeze for the White House's senior officials, the roughly one hundred people who earned more than a hundred thousand dollars a year, saying that "families are tightening their belts, and so should Washington." It was a small but visible gesture of sharing the struggle with the American people during hard times.

A more dramatic move would have been for Obama himself to refuse to accept the president's four-hundred-thousand-dollar annual salary and to work instead for a token sum of one dollar a year. (He could afford it: he was already a multimillionaire from the sales of his two best-selling books.) During World War II Goldman Sachs's chief, Sidney Weinberg, had rallied many of his fellow corporate leaders to come to Washington and work as so-called dollar-a-year men. Senior executives from General Electric, General Motors, Ford Motor, and Sears, Roebuck all signed up. They provided public service without seeking any personal profit during a time of national crisis. In that era, corporate higher-ups got rich from their salaries, not primarily from lucrative stock options, as they do today, so forgoing private-sector paychecks back then was much more of a sacrifice than it would be now.

For Obama to have proclaimed himself a dollar-a-year man would have been an impressive action. Nonetheless, his smaller gesture did matter, especially since it came at a time of incredible irresponsibility among those who were supposed to be leaders. The following day, the news broke that John Thain, the chief of the Wall Street firm Merrill Lynch, had spent $1.22 million of the company's money redecorating his office and conference rooms—including $87,000 for a rug—and had pushed his board to approve his own $30 million bonus while he laid off thousands of workers. Even though he knew that Merrill was about to declare a $15 billion quarterly loss, he had issued billions of dollars in secret last-minute bonuses to his senior executives, sticking the federal government's bailout program with the huge costs. In that context, Obama's moves to limit the salaries of his top officials—and to close the "revolving door" that would have let them profit mightily from their connections—were significant.

In addition to sharing the struggle, Obama's way of walking the walk included getting a firsthand view of what was happening out "there" in the nation he was trying to lead. That's an extremely hard challenge for any American president, who must exist constantly within the bubble of Secret Service security as well as the echo chamber of his close-knit cadre of advisers and gatekeepers. Franklin Delano Roosevelt, who was further hindered by the immobility of his crippled legs, relied on his First Lady to be his "eyes and ears" as she traveled widely; she was known as "Eleanor Everywhere." Obama, for his part, shrewdly fought for and won approval from his security handlers to keep a strongly encrypted version of his BlackBerry, which would enable him to stay in touch constantly through e-mail with dozens of old friends who could be his eyes and ears on America beyond the bubble.

In his first days in office, Obama also sought the firsthand view by hosting an open house for two hundred citizens (who had signed up on a first-come, first-served basis) and by making a surprise visit to the White House press room. When he saw the cramped space where the correspondents worked, he commented, "I gotta say, it's smaller than I thought." And he remarked on the need for healthier snacks than the junk food in their vending machines. The visit showed that he cared about their day-to-day well-being. But he should have gone further and showed that he cared deeply about their opinions and strove to see through their eyes. One of the reporters took advantage of the casual visit to question Obama about his first noticeable failure to walk the walk: his appointee for deputy secretary of defense would need a waiver from Obama's executive order against lobbyists becoming government officials. Obama was taken aback and refused to answer. He even reacted defensively by making an open threat: "I can't come in and shake hands if I'm going to get grilled every time," he said. That seemed a regrettable response. But perhaps hearing the question in a behind-the-scenes, close-up, face-to-face, eye-to-eye encounter would prove more persuasive to Obama than fielding it in the formal public showcase of a televised press conference. Everyone is always watching to see how the leader walks the walk, but few people have the access or the temerity to confront him when he's failing to walk it. Obama's first days as president showed a strong intuitive grasp of the demands of leadership, but even he will need to seek out those who speak truth to his power.

As Obama took office, the nation desperately needed his leadership, but it also needed the heads of its most influential corporations to change dramatically. America had a new president whose confidence recalled FDR's in the Great Depression, but it still lacked corporate leaders like the best ones from that era. We needed leaders reminiscent of General Electric's longtime president Gerard Swope, who was an influential force behind the passage of the Social Security Act of 1935, the first legislation to bring pensions and unemployment insurance to the masses. While the automakers and steelmakers fought bitterly (and

sometimes violently) to keep out the unions, Swope *invited* them
to organize GE's hourly workers. It was no wonder that his company avoided the labor unrest—including the bloody strikes and
the factory sit-ins and occupations—that shook other major U.S.
industrial companies in the late 1930s.

As the Obama era began during soaring unemployment,
American business needed leaders in the mold of IBM's legendary
Thomas J. Watson Sr., who risked bankruptcy rather than lay off
a single one of his employees during the Great Depression. During Obama's first week as president, when people gasped over the
revelations about John Thain's million-dollar office redecoration,
far fewer raised eyebrows when Microsoft—one of the greatest
wealth machines in recent history—announced that it was laying
off five thousand of its ninety-four thousand workers. Microsoft
had produced three decabillionaires—including its current chief
executive officer, Steve Ballmer—and it still held $20 billion in
cash from profits generated by its near-monopolistic position during better times. That great pile of cash worked out to $4 million
left in the bank for every employee being laid off. If Microsoft
wouldn't stick by its people during harder times, who would? If
Microsoft wouldn't take its place as today's successor to enlightened corporations like the GE and the IBM of the '30s, who
would?

In his inaugural address, President Obama called for "a new
era of responsibility." For would-be corporate leaders, the meaning was all too clear:

Enough!

The time had finally come to walk the walk.

For their unflagging support, enthusiasm, energy, insight, and good judgment, I'm so grateful to Adrian Zackheim, Courtney Young, Will Weisser, and Allison Sweet McLean at Portfolio; Eric Lupfer and Suzanne Gluck at William Morris Endeavor; and especially my wife, Susan Rebecca White.

Chapter One | When You Walk the Walk,
You Show What's Really Most Important

pg. 2 **On the Nazi's attack on Martin Luther King Jr.:** Taylor Branch, *Parting the Waters: America in the King Years 1954–1963* (New York: Simon & Schuster, 1988); David J. Garrow, *Bearing the Cross: Martin Luther King Jr. and the Southern Christian Leadership Conference* (New York: HarperCollins, 2004); Peter Kihss, "Dr. King Assaulted by Self-Styled American Nazi," *New York Times*, September 29, 1962. An Associated Press story ran in two somewhat different versions as "White 'Nazi' Slugs King in Alabama" in the *Washington Post* and as "American Nazi Hits Rev. King; Fined, Jailed" in the *Chicago Tribune*, both on September 29, 1962.

pg. 6 **On John Rawls and "first virtues":** Amy Gutman, "A Life That Sought Justice," *Princeton Alumni Weekly*, January 29, 2003.

pg. 6 **On the Rule of One or Two:** Peter Drucker said in an interview with Rich Karlgaard, "Peter Drucker on Leadership," *Forbes*, November 19, 2004: "When you are the chief executive . . . develop your priorities and don't have more than two. I don't know anybody who can do three things at the same time and do them well. Do one task at a time or two tasks at a time. That's it." Similarly, in Drucker's "Six Rules for Presidents," in *Managing in a Time of Great Change* (New York: Dutton, 1995), he writes: "There are usually a half-dozen right answers to 'What needs to be done?' Yet unless a president makes the risky and controversial choice of only one, he will achieve nothing."

pg. 9 **On Coca-Cola executive Muhtar Kent's insider trading scandal:** Chad Terhune, "Coke May Tap Kent as No. 2, Despite Insider Trading Past," *Wall Street Journal*, January 19, 2006; Colin Barr, "The Five Dumbest Things on Wall Street This Week," *The Street*, January 20, 2006, http://www.thestreet.com.

Chapter Two | When You Walk the Walk, You Show Who Comes First

pg. 15 **On Jeff Bezos and Amazon.com:** Alan Deutschman, "Inside the Mind of Jeff Bezos," *Fast Company*, August 2004; Gary Rivlin, "A Retail Revolution Turns 10, *New York Times*, July 10, 2005.

pg. 22 **On Sidney Weinberg and Goldman Sachs:** Lisa Endlich, *Goldman Sachs: The Culture of Success* (New York: Touchstone, 2000); *Time*, "Everybody's Broker Sidney Weinberg," December 8, 1958.

pg. 26 **On Herb Kelleher and Southwest:** Kevin Freiberg and Jackie Freiberg, *Nuts!: Southwest Airlines' Crazy Recipe for Business and Personal Success* (New York: Broadway, 1998); Jody Hoffer Gittell, *The Southwest Airlines Way: Using the Power of Relationships to Achieve High Performance* (New York: McGraw-Hill, 2003); Joe Nocera, "The Sinatra of Southwest Feels the Love," *New York Times*, May 24, 2008; Micheline Maynard, "Southwest Turns a Profit for 69th Straight Quarter," *New York Times*, July 25, 2008.

pg. 28 **On Frank Lorenzo and Continental and the lemmingship of airline CEOs:** Eric Weiner, "Lorenzo, Head of Continental Air, Quits Industry in $30 Million Deal," *New York Times*, August 10, 1990; "Payday for CEOs," *Bill Moyers Journal*, June 6, 2007, http://www.pbs.org; *Business Week*, "Reading a CEO's Paycheck," April 25, 2003; Chris Isidore, "Northwest Files for Bankruptcy," *CNN Money*, September

14, 2005, http://www.cnnmoney.com. **Continental flight attendant Cara Winkler's quote:** *The NewsHour with Jim Lehrer,* March 19, 1998, http://www.pbs.org.

pg. 33 **On Danny Meyer and the Union Square Cafe:** Danny Meyer, *Setting the Table: The Transforming Power of Hospitality in Business* (New York: HarperCollins, 2006); Winnie Hu and Ann Farmer, "The Smoking Ban," *New York Times,* December 28, 2003.

pgs. 35–39 **On Masaru Ibuka and Sony:** John Nathan, *Sony: The Private Life* (Boston: Houghton Mifflin, 1999). **Ibuka's obituary:** James Sterngold, "Masaru Ibuka, 89, Engineer and Sony Co-Founder, Dies," *New York Times,* December 20, 1997. **Ibuka's quote on Trinitron as his favorite Sony product:** interview with Brenton R. Schlender, "The Real Genius Behind Sony," *Fortune,* February 24, 1992. **The Sony "Founding Prospectus":** reprinted in English translation on the company's Web site, http://www.sony.net. **For figures on color TV sales and the number of percentage of TV households in the United States:** http://www.tv.history/tv.

Chapter Three | When You Walk the Walk,
You Show What Comes First

pg. 41 **On Ray Kroc and McDonald's:** John F. Love, *McDonald's: Behind the Arches* (New York: Bantam, 1995); Martin S. Meyers and Scott Wallace, "Factors Influencing the Purchasing of Fast Food Meals," *Proceedings of the Academy of Marketing Studies,* 8, no. 2 (2003).

pg. 44 **On Fred Smith and FedEx:** Vance Trimble, *Overnight Success: Federal Express & Frederick Smith, Its Renegade Creator* (New York: Crown, 1993); Frederick W. Smith, "Competing with the Postal Service," *Cato Policy Report,* March–April 1999.

pg. 46 **On Charles Schwab:** John Kador, *Charles Schwab: How*

One Company Beat Wall Street and Reinvented the Brokerage Industry (New York: John Wiley, 2002).

pg. 49 **On Enterprise Rent-A-Car:** Alex Frankel, *Punching In: The Unauthorized Adventures of a Front-Line Employee* (New York: Collins, 2007).

pg. 50 **On Howard Schultz and Starbucks:** Taylor Clark, *Starbucked: A Double Tall Tale of Caffeine, Commerce, and Culture* (New York: Little, Brown, 2007).

pg. 52 **On Eleanor Roosevelt:** Blanche Wiesen Cook, *Eleanor Roosevelt: Volume 1, 1884–1993* (New York: Viking Penguin, 1992) and *Eleanor Roosevelt: Volume 2, The Defining Years, 1933–1938* (New York: Penguin Books, 1999); Mary Ann Glendon, *A World Made New: Eleanor Roosevelt and the Universal Declaration of Human Rights* (New York: Random House, 2001).

pg. 54 **On Nelson Mandela:** Anthony Sampson, *Mandela: The Authorized Biography* (New York: Vintage Books, 2000); John Carlin, *Playing the Enemy: Nelson Mandela and the Game That Made a Nation* (New York: Penguin Press, 2008).

Chapter Four | When You Walk the Walk,
You Share the Struggle and the Risk

pg. 61 **On Bill Hewlett and Hewlett-Packard:** Michael S. Malone, *Bill & Dave: How Hewlett and Packard Built the World's Greatest Company* (New York: Portfolio Books, 2007).

pg. 61 **On the 1970 recession:** "1970: The Year of the Hangover," *Time*, December 28, 1970.

pg. 65 **On Al Gore's Nashville home:** Gregg Easterbrook. "Al Gore's Outsourcing Solutions," *New York Times*, March 9, 2007; David Remnick, "The Wilderness Campaign," *New Yorker*, September

13, 2004; Tom Zeller Jr., "An Inconveniently Easy Headline: Gore's Electric Bills Spark Debate," *New York Times*, February 28, 2007; Eric Schelzig, "Gore Goes Green, Making Changes to Nashville House," Associated Press, June 10, 2007; Kristin M. Hall, "Group: Gore a Hypocrite over Power Bill," Associated Press, February 28, 2007; Ed Pilkington, "An Inconvenient Truth: Eco-warrior Al Gore's Bloated Gas and Electricity Bills," *Guardian*, February 28, 2007; Felicity Barringer and Andrew C. Revkin, "Gore Warns Congressional Panels of 'Planetary Emergency' on Global Warming," *New York Times*, March 22, 2007.

pg. 66 **On Laura Turner Seydel and the "EcoManor":** Patricia Sellars, "The First Certifiably Green Mansion," *Fortune*, March 19, 2007; Alma E. Hill, "Building Green: 'EcoManor' Makes an Earth-Friendly Statement," *Atlanta Journal-Constitution*, February 1, 2007.

pg. 67 **On Mark Fields and Ford Motor:** Micheline Maynard, "After Inquiries, Ford Official Decides to Skip Company Jet," *New York Times*, January 19, 2007; Micheline Maynard, "Is There a Ford in Ford's Future," *New York Times*, January 8, 2006; Nick Bunkley, "Ford Pays Chief $28 Million for 4 Months' Work," *New York Times*, April 6, 2007; Micheline Maynard and Nick Bunkley, "Ford Chief Sticking to His Road Map for Turnaround," *New York Times*, April 5, 2007.

pg. 69 **On commanders sharing the struggle and risk throughout the history of warfare:** John Keegan, *The Mask of Command* (New York: Penguin Books, 1988).

pg. 70 **Translation of Alexander the Great's speech:** Waldemar Heckel and John Yardley, *Alexander the Great: Historical Sources in Translation* (Malden, MA: Blackwell Publishing, 2004).

pg. 72 **On George Washington:** Joseph J. Ellis, *His Excellency:*

George Washington (New York: Vintage Books, 2005); James R. Gaines, *For Liberty and Glory: Washington, Lafayette, and Their Revolutions* (New York: Norton, 2007).

pgs. 75, 77 **Lord Moran's memoir of World War I:** *The Anatomy of Courage* (New York: Carroll & Graf, 2007), and **his memoir of Winston Churchill:** *Churchill at War: 1940–45* (New York: Carroll & Graf, 2003).

pg. 77 **On World War II commanders Robert Eichelberger and Lucian Truscott:** Cole C. Kingseed, *Old Glory Stories: American Combat Leadership in World War II* (Annapolis, MD: Naval Institute Press, 2006).

pg. 79 **On the war's soldiers and their attitude toward leadership:** Gerald F. Linderman, *The World Within War: America's Combat Experience in World War II* (Cambridge, MA: Harvard University Press, 1997).

pg. 80 **General H. Norman Schwarzkopf's memoir (with Peter Petre):** *It Doesn't Take a Hero* (New York: Bantam, 1993).

pg. 85 **On A. P. Giannini and Bank of America:** Moira Johnson, *The Tumultuous History of the Bank of America* (Washington, DC: Beard Books, 2000).

pg. 86 **On Sam Walton and Wal-Mart:** Vance H. Trimble, *Sam Walton: The Inside Story of America's Richest Man* (New York: Dutton, 1990).

pg. 87 **On Alice Waters and Chez Panisse:** Thomas McNamee, *Alice Waters and Chez Panisse: The Romantic, Impractical, Often Eccentric, Ultimately Brilliant Making of a Food Revolution* (New York: Penguin Books, 2008).

pg. 87 **On Whole Foods:** I've changed the names to protect the privacy of the individuals.

pg. 91 **On Warren Buffett:** Roger Lowenstein, *Buffett: The Making of an American Capitalist* (New York: Broadway Books, 2001).

Chapter Five | When You Walk the Walk, You Gain a Firsthand View

pg. 93 **On Michael Bloomberg:** Michael N. Grynbaum, "Mayor Takes the Subway—By Way of S.U.V.," *New York Times*, August 1, 2007.

pg. 95 **On Fiorello LaGuardia:** Alyn Brodsky, *The Great Mayor: Fiorello LaGuardia and the Making of the City of New York* (New York: St. Martin's Press, 2003); Melvin G. Holli, *The American Mayor: The Best & the Worst Big-City Leaders* (University Park: Pennsylvania State University Press, 1999).

pg. 100 **Walter Bedell Smith's quote on the American generals not believing the challenge of the bocage country:** S. L. A. Marshall, *Men Against Fire: The Problem of Battle Command* (Norman: University of Oklahoma Press, 2000).

pg. 103 **On Howard Schulz visiting thirty to forty Starbucks a week:** William Meyers, "Conscience in a Cup of Coffee," *U.S. News & World Report*, July 18, 2007.

Chapter Six | When You Walk the Walk, Every Moment Is an Opportunity to Teach, Train, and Lead

pg. 109 **On General George Custer's red necktie:** Stephen A. Ambrose, *Crazy Horse and Custer: The Parallel Lives of Two American Warriors* (New York: Anchor Books, 1996).

pg. 111 **On Steve Jobs's field trip to Fallingwater:** Alan Deutschman, *The Second Coming of Steve Jobs* (New York: Broadway Books, 2000).

pg. 112 **Robert Mondavi's memoir:** *Harvests of Joy: How the Good Life Became Great Business* (New York: Harcourt, Brace, 1998).

pg. 114 **On Jack Welch recruiting the auto mechanic:** Jack Welch, with John A. Byrne, *Jack: Straight from the Gut* (New York: Warner Books, 2001).

Chapter Seven | When You Walk the Walk, You Take Steps That Every Potential Follower Can Follow

pg. 121 **On the Greensboro Four:** Mark Kurlansky, *1968: The Year That Rocked the World* (New York: Random House, 2005); Howard Zinn, *The Zinn Reader: Writings on Disobedience and Democracy* (New York: Seven Stories, 1997).

pg. 123 **On Arnold Schwarzenegger and his Hummers:** Medea Benjamin, "An Earth Day Call to Arnold Schwarzenegger: Go Hummer Free," *Common Dreams,* April 22, 2004, http://www .commondreams.org; Carla Marinucci, "Humm Baby, Schwarzenegger Keeping His Hummers," *San Francisco Gate,* September 22, 2006, http://www.sfgate.com.

pg. 125 **On Al Gore's "green" home remodeling:** Erik Schelzig, "Gore Makes His Mansion Greener," Associated Press, December 14, 2007.

Chapter Eight | When You Walk the Walk, You Become a Leader Even Without the Title, Position, or Formal Authority

pg. 134 **On Urban Meyer and University of Florida football:** Austin Murphy, "Comeback Gators," *Sports Illustrated,* December 15, 2008; and Stewart Mandel, "Tebow Enhances Legend in Victory," *Sports Illustrated,* December 6, 2008, http://www.si.com.

pg. 137 **On Pixar:** Ed Catmull, "How Pixar Fosters Collective Creativity," *Harvard Business Review,* September 2008.

Chapter Nine | When You Walk the Walk, You Inspire Belief

pg. 141 **On the Fremont, California, auto factory:** Paul Ingrassia and Joseph B. White, *Comeback: The Fall & Rise of the American Automobile Industry* (New York: Simon & Schuster, 1994); and Maryann Keller, *Rude Awakening: The Rise, Fall, and Struggle for Recovery of General Motors* (New York: William Morrow, 1989).

pg. 146 **On Wendy Kopp and Teach for America:** Wendy Kopp, "Teaching as Leadership: Lessons from Teach for America," in *The College Board Review,* Spring 2008; Jeffrey Kluger, "Wendy Kopp," *Time,* May 10, 2008; "Alumni Who Changed America, and the World," *Princeton Alumni Weekly,* January 23, 2008.

pg. 153 **On KIPP and Delancey Street Foundation:** Alan Deutschman, *Change or Die: The Three Keys to Change at Work and in Life* (New York: HarperCollins, 2008).

Afterword | A Week of Walking the Walk

pg. 167 **On White House residence's lights at 5:00 a.m.:** "Obama— The First 100 Hours," *Guardian,* January 24, 2009.

pg. 168 **On Bush's unprecedented expansion of presidential power:** Charlie Savage, "Bush Challenges Hundreds of Laws," *Boston Globe,* April 30, 2006; Elizabeth Drew, "Power Grab," *New York Review of Books,* June 22, 2006.

pg. 170 **On the "mockery of due process":** "First Steps at Guantanamo," *New York Times,* January 21, 2009.

pg. 171 **On Clinton's support for NAFTA undermining his health-care reform initiative:** John McGregor Burns and Georgia J. Sorenson, *Dead Center: Clinton-Gore Leadership and the Perils of Moderation* (New York: Scribner, 1999).

pg. 172 **On Eisenhower as "almost criminal":** Stephen E. Ambrose,

Eisenhower: Soldier and President (New York: Simon & Schuster, 1991).

pg. *173* **On "dollar-a-year" men:** Daniel Gross, "Tech's Phony Dollar-a-Year Men," *Slate,* January 30, 2003, http://www.slate.com.

pg. *175* **On Gerard Swope:** William E. Rothschild, *The Secret to GE's Success* (New York: McGraw-Hill, 2007).